Back to Basics: Home Buying & Selling

by Eric Tyson and Ray Brown

WILEY

Publisher's Acknowledgments

Editorial Project Manager:
Victoria M. Adang

Senior Acquisitions Editor:
Tracy Boggier

Production Editor:
Siddique Shaik

Cover Images: (for sale sign)
© jamtoons / Getty Images,
(percent sign) © jamtoons /
Getty Images

Cover Design: Wiley

Back to Basics: Home Buying & Selling

Published by John Wiley & Sons, Inc.
111 River St.
Hoboken, NJ 07030-5774
http://www.wiley.com
Copyright © 2018 by Eric Tyson and Ray Brown

For general information on our other products and services, please contact our Business Development Department in the U.S. at 317-572-3205.

ISBN 978-1-119-47260-5 (pbk); ISBN 978-1-119-47296-4 (ePub); ISBN 978-1-119-47297-1 (ePDF)

Manufactured in the United States of America

10 9 8 7 6 5 4 3 2 1

Contents

1

Deciding Whether to Buy

Buying a home may well be the largest purchase you ever make. Buying a home can send shock waves through your personal finances and may even cause a sleepless night or two. Purchasing a home is a major financial step and a life event for most people. You owe it to yourself to do things right.

This chapter gives you a quick overview of the advantages of buying a house versus renting a place to call home. Homeownership isn't for everyone. In this chapter, we help you determine whether home buying is right for you.

Ownership Advantages

Most people should eventually buy homes, but not all people and not at every point in their lives. To decide whether now's the time for you to buy, consider the advantages of buying and whether they apply to you.

Owning should be less expensive than renting

Most of us take shelter for granted, unless we don't have it or are confronted for the first time with paying for it ourselves. Remember your first apartment when you graduated from college or when your folks finally pushed you out of the nest? That place probably made you appreciate the good deal you had before — even those cramped college dorms may have seemed more attractive!

But even if you pay several hundred to a thousand dollars or more per month in rent, that expense may not seem so steep if you happen to peek at a home for sale. In most parts of the United States, we're talking about a big number — $150,000, $225,000, $350,000, or more for the sticker price.

Here's a guideline that may change the way you view your seemingly cheap monthly rent. To figure out the price of a home you could buy for approximately the same monthly cost as your current rent, simply do the following calculation:

Take your monthly rent and multiply by 200, and you come up with the purchase price of a home.

$ _____ per month × 200 = $ _____

Example: $1,000×200=$200,000

If you were paying rent of $1,000 per month, you would pay approximately the same amount per month to own a $200,000 home (factoring in tax savings). Now your monthly rent doesn't sound quite so cheap compared with the cost of buying a home, does it? (We show you how to accurately calculate the total costs of owning a home in Chapter 2.)

Even more important than the cost *today* of buying versus renting is the cost in the *future*. As a renter, your rent is fully exposed to increases in the cost of living, also known as *inflation*. A reasonable expectation for annual increases in your rent is 4 percent per year.

_____

_____

_____

When you're in your 20s or 30s, you may not be thinking or caring about your golden years, but your rent skyrockets over the decades ahead with modest inflation! Paying $1,000 rent per month now is the equivalent of buying a home for $200,000. In 40 years, with 4 percent inflation per year, your $1,000-per-month rent will balloon to $4,800 per month. That's like buying a house for $960,000!

In our example, we picked $1,000 for rent to show you what happens to that rent with a modest 4 percent annual rate of inflation. To see what may happen to your current rent at that rate of inflation, simply complete Table 1-1.

Your Current Monthly Rent	Multiplication Factor to Determine Rent in Future Years at 4 Percent Annual Inflation Rate	Projected Future Rent
$_____	× 1.48	= $_____ in 10 years
$_____	× 2.19	= $_____ in 20 years
$_____	× 3.24	= $_____ in 30 years
$_____	× 4.80	= $_____ in 40 years
$_____	× 7.11	= $_____ in 50 years
$_____	× 10.52	= $_____ in 60 years

Table 1-1: *Figuring Future Rent*

Although the cost of purchasing a home generally increases over the years, after you purchase a home, the bulk of your housing costs aren't exposed to inflation if you use a fixed-rate mortgage to finance the purchase. As we explain in Chapter 5, a *fixed-rate mortgage* locks your mortgage payment in at a fixed amount (as opposed to an adjustable-rate mortgage payment that fluctuates in value with changes in interest rates). Therefore, only the comparatively smaller property taxes, insurance, and maintenance expenses will increase over time with inflation. (In Chapter 2, we cover what buying and owning a home costs.)

You're always going to need a place to live. And over the long term, inflation has almost always been around. Even if you must stretch a little to buy a home today, in the decades ahead, you'll be glad you did. The financial danger with renting long term is that *all* of your housing costs (rent) increase over time. We're not saying that everyone should buy because of inflation, but we do think that if you're not going to buy, you should be careful to plan your finances accordingly.

You can make your house your own

Think back to all the places you ever rented, including the rental in which you may currently be living. For each unit,

_____

_____

_____

make a list of the things you would have changed if the property were yours: ugly carpeting, yucky exterior paint job, outdated appliances that didn't work well, and so on.

Although we know some tenants who do some work on their own apartments, we don't generally endorse this approach because it takes your money and time but financially benefits the building's owner.

When you own your own place, however, you can do whatever you want to it. Want hardwood floors instead of green shag carpeting? Tear it out. Love neon-orange carpeting and pink exterior paint? You can add it!

In your zest and enthusiasm to buy a place and make it your own, be careful of two things:

- **Don't make the place too weird.** You'll probably want or need to sell your home someday, and the more outrageous you make it, the fewer buyers it will appeal to — and the lower the price it will likely fetch. If you don't mind throwing money away or are convinced that you can find a buyer with similar tastes, be as weird as you want. If you do make improvements, focus on those that add value: skylights, a deck addition for an outdoor living area, updated kitchens and bathrooms, and so on.

- **Beware of running yourself into financial ruin.** Improvements and remodeling cost money. Some home buyers neglect other important financial goals (such as saving for retirement and their kids' college costs) in order to endlessly renovate their homes. Others rack up significant debts that hang like financial weights over their heads. In the worst cases, homes become money pits that cause owners to build up high-interest consumer debt as a prelude to bankruptcy or foreclosure.

You avoid unpleasant landlords

A final benefit of owning your own home is that you don't have to subject yourself to the whims of a landlord. Much is made among real estate investors of the challenges of finding good tenants. As a tenant, perhaps you've already discovered that finding a good landlord isn't easy, either.

The fundamental problem with some landlords is that they're slow to fix problems and make improvements. The best (and smartest) landlords realize that keeping the building shipshape helps attract and keep good tenants and maximizes rents and profits. But to some landlords, maximizing profits means being stingy with repairs and improvements.

When you own your home, the good news is that you're generally in control — you can get your stopped-up toilet fixed or your ugly walls painted whenever you like. No more hassling with unresponsive landlords. The bad news is that you're responsible for paying for and ensuring completion of the work. Even if you hire someone else to do it, you still must find competent contractors and oversee their work, neither of which is an easy responsibility.

Another risk of renting is that landlords may decide to sell the building and put you out on the street. You should ask your prospective landlords whether they have plans to sell. Some landlords won't give you a truthful answer, but the question is worth asking if this issue is a concern to you.

Renting Advantages

Buying and owning a home throughout most of your adult life makes good financial and personal sense for most people — but not all people and not at all times. Renting works better for some people. The benefits of renting are many:

_____

_____

_____

- **Simplicity:** Yes, searching for a rental unit that meets your needs can take more than a few days (especially if you're in a tight rental market), but it should be easier than finding a place to buy. When you buy, you must line up financing, conduct inspections, and deal with myriad other issues that renters never have to face. When you do it right, finding and buying a good home can be a time-consuming process.

- **Convenience:** After you find and move into your rental, your landlord is responsible for the never-ending task of property maintenance and upkeep. Buildings and appliances age, and bad stuff happens: Fuses blow, plumbing backs up, heaters break in the middle of winter, roofs spring leaks during record-breaking rainfalls, trees come crashing down during windstorms. The list goes on and on. As a renter, you can leave all of these concerns to someone else.

- **Flexibility:** You may be one of those people who dislikes feeling tied down. With a rental, as long as your lease allows (and most leases don't run longer than a year), you can move on. As a homeowner, if you want to move, you must sell your home or find a tenant to rent it.

- **Increased liquidity:** Unless you're the beneficiary of a large inheritance or work at a high-paying job, you'll probably be financially stretched when you buy your first home. Coming up with the down payment and closing costs usually cleans out most people's financial reserves. In addition, when you buy a home, you must meet your monthly mortgage payments, property taxes, insurance, and maintenance and repair expenses. As a renter, you can keep your extra cash; budgeting is also easier without the upkeep-expense surprises that home-owners experience, such as the need to replace a leaking roof or old furnace.

  You don't need to buy a home to cut your taxes. Should you have access to a retirement account such as a 401(k), 403(b), or SEP-IRA, you can cut your taxes while you save and invest your extra cash as a renter. So saving on taxes shouldn't be the sole motivation for you to buy a home.

- **Better diversification:** Many homeowners who are financially stretched have the bulk of their wealth tied up in their homes. As a renter, you can invest your money in a variety of sound investments, such as stocks, bonds, and perhaps your own small business. Over the long term, the stock market has produced comparable rates of return to investing in the real estate market.

- **Maybe lower cost:** If you live in an area where home prices have risen much faster than rental rates, real estate may be overpriced and not a good buy.

Renting should also be cheaper than buying if you expect to move soon. Buying and selling property costs big bucks. With real estate agent commissions, loan fees, title insurance, inspections, and all sorts of other costs, your property must appreciate approximately 15 percent just for you to break even and recoup these costs. Therefore, buying property that you don't expect to hold onto for at least three (and preferably five or more) years doesn't make much economic sense. Although you may sometimes experience appreciation in excess of 15 percent over a year or two, most of the time you won't. If you're counting on such high appreciation, you're setting yourself up for disappointment.

2

Calculating Homeownership Costs

Most home buyers must finance their purchase — so they allow a banker or other lender to determine how much home they can afford. Such determinations are based on a buyer's income and other debt obligations.

But here's where most people get confused. When a lender says you qualify to borrow, say, $200,000 for a house, this doesn't mean you can *afford* to spend that much on a house. What the lender is effectively saying to you is, "Based on what little I know about your situation and the fact that I can't control your future behavior, this is the maximum amount that I think is a prudent risk for my organization to lend to you."

The lender normally requires a certain down payment to protect itself against the possibility that you may default on the loan. Should you default on a mortgage, for example, the lender will foreclose on the property. This process takes time and money.

In this chapter, we help you determine what you can comfortably afford to spend on a home as well as how to calculate how much a particular home is likely to cost you.

Lenders Can't Tell You What You Can Afford

Ultimately, a lender doesn't care about you, your financial situation, or your other needs as long as it has protected its financial interests. The lender doesn't know or care whether you're

- Falling behind in saving for retirement

- Wanting to save money for other important financial goals, such as starting or buying your own small business

- Parenting several kids (or facing private-schooling costs)

- Lacking proper personal insurance protection

And therein lies the problem of deciding how much home you can afford to buy on the basis of how much money a lender is willing to lend you.

People at all income levels can get into trouble and over-extend themselves by purchasing more house than they can afford and by taking on more debt than they can handle. Just because a lender or real estate agent says you're eligible for, or can qualify for, a certain size loan doesn't mean that's what you can afford given your personal financial situation. Lenders *can't* tell you what you can afford — they can tell you *only* the maximum that they'll allow you to borrow.

The Cost of Buying and Owning a Home

Before you set out in search of your dream home, one of the single most important questions you should answer is, "What can I afford to spend on a home?" To answer that question intelligently, you first need to understand what your financial goals are, what it will take to achieve them, and where you are today. (If you need help setting financial goals, pick up a copy of Eric's *Back to Basics: Personal Finance* [Wiley].) In the following sections, we dig into the costs of buying and owning a home.

Mortgage payments

In Chapter 5, we discuss selecting the best type of mortgage that fits your particular circumstances. In the meantime, you must still confront mortgages because mortgages constitute the biggest component of the total cost of owning a home.

Start with the basics: A *mortgage* is a loan you take out to buy a home. A mortgage allows you to purchase a $150,000 home even though you have far less money than that to put toward the purchase.

With few exceptions, mortgage loans in the United States are typically repaid over a 15- or 30-year time span. Almost all mortgages require monthly payments. Here's how a mortgage works. Suppose you're purchasing a $150,000 home and you have saved a 20 percent ($30,000, in this example) down payment. Thus, you're in the market for a $120,000 mortgage.

You sit down with a mortgage lender who asks you to complete a stack of paperwork. Just when you think the worst is over, the lender gives you an even bigger headache by talking about the hundreds of mortgage options.

Don't worry — we can help you cut through the clutter! Imagine, for a moment, a simple world where the mortgage lender offers you only two mortgage options: a 15-year fixed-rate mortgage and a 30-year fixed-rate mortgage (*fixed-rate* simply means that the interest rate on the loan stays fixed and level over the life of the loan). Here's what your monthly payment would be under each mortgage option:

$120,000, 15-year mortgage @ 7.00 percent = $1,079 per month

$120,000, 30-year mortgage @ 7.25 percent = $819 per month

As we discuss in Chapter 5, the interest rate is typically a little bit lower on a 15-year mortgage versus a 30-year mortgage because shorter-term loans are a little less risky for lenders. Note how much higher the monthly payment is on the 15-year mortgage than on the 30-year mortgage. Your payments must be higher for the 15-year mortgage because you're paying off the same size loan 15 years faster.

But don't let the higher monthly payments on the 15-year loan cause you to forget that at the end of 15 years, your mortgage payments disappear, whereas with the 30-year mortgage, you still have 15 more years' worth of monthly payments to go. So although you have a higher required monthly payment with the 15-year mortgage, check out the difference in the total payments and interest on the two mortgage options:

Mortgage Option	Total Payments	Total Interest
15-year mortgage	$194,147	$74,147
30-year mortgage	$294,700	$174,700

Note: In case you're curious about how we got the total interest amount, we simply subtracted the amount of the loan repaid ($120,000) from the "Total Payments." Also, the monthly payment numbers previously cited, as well as these total payments and interest numbers, are rounded off, so if you try multiplying 180 or 360 by the monthly payment numbers, you won't get answers identical to these numbers.

With the 30-year mortgage (compared with the 15-year mortgage), because you're borrowing the money over 15 additional years, it shouldn't come as a great surprise that you end up paying more than \$100,000 additional interest. The 30-year loan isn't necessarily inferior; its lower payments may better allow you to accomplish other important financial goals, such as saving in a tax-deductible retirement account.

In the early years of repaying your mortgage, nearly all of your mortgage payment goes toward paying interest on the money that you borrowed. Not until the later years of your mortgage do you begin to rapidly pay down your loan balance.

Lender's limits

Because we've personally seen the financial consequences of people borrowing too much (yet still staying within the boundaries of what mortgage lenders allow), you won't hear us saying in this section that lenders can tell you the amount you can afford to spend on a home. They can't. All mortgage lenders can do is tell you their criteria for approving and denying mortgage applications and calculating the maximum that you're eligible to borrow. (For information on lenders and their limits, see the first section of this chapter.)

Mortgage lenders tally up your monthly *housing expense*, the components of which they consider to be

	Mortgage payment	(*PI* for principal and interest)
+	Property taxes	(*T* for taxes)
+	Insurance	(*I* for insurance)
=	Lender's definition of *housing expense*	(PITI is the common acronym)

For a given property that you're considering buying, a mortgage lender calculates the housing expense and normally requires that it not exceed a certain percentage (typically around 40 percent or so) of your monthly before-tax *(gross)* income. So, for example, if your monthly gross income is $6,000, your lender will not allow your expected monthly housing expense to exceed $2,400 (if the lender is using 40 percent). When you're self-employed and complete IRS Form 1040, Schedule C, mortgage lenders use your after-expenses *(net)* income, from the bottom line of Schedule C.

This housing-expense ratio ignores almost all of your other financial goals, needs, and obligations. It also ignores utilities, maintenance, and remodeling expenses, which can consume a lot of a homeowner's cash.

About the only other financial considerations a lender takes into account (besides your income) are your other debts.

Specifically, mortgage lenders examine the required monthly payments for student loans, an auto loan, credit card bills, and other debts. In addition to the percentage of your income lenders allow for housing expenses, lenders typically allow an additional 5 percent of your monthly income to go toward other debt repayments. Thus, your monthly housing expense and monthly repayment of nonhousing debts can total up to, but generally be no more than, 45 percent.

Figuring the size of your mortgage payments

Calculating the size of your mortgage payment, after you know the amount you want to borrow, is simple. The hard part for most people is determining how much they can afford to borrow.

Suppose you calculate that you can afford to spend $1,500 per month on housing. Determining the exact amount of mortgage that allows you to stay within this boundary is a little challenging because the housing cost you figure that you can afford ($1,500, in our example) is made up of several components: mortgage payments, property taxes, insurance, and maintenance. (Note that although lenders don't care about maintenance expenses in figuring what you can afford to buy, you shouldn't overlook this significant expense.)

As you change the amount that you're willing to spend on a home, the size of the mortgage you choose to take out also usually changes, but so do the other property cost components. So you may have to play with the numbers a bit to get them to work out just right. You may pick a certain home and then figure the property taxes, insurance, maintenance, and the like. When you tally everything, you may find that the total comes in above or below your desired target. If you come out a little high, you need to cut back a bit and choose a slightly less-costly property and/or get a smaller mortgage.

Using Table 2-1, you can calculate the size of your mortgage payments based on the amount you want to borrow, the loan's interest rate, and the length (in years) the mortgage payments last. To determine the monthly payment on a mortgage, simply multiply the relevant number from Table 2-1 by the size of your mortgage expressed in (divided by) thousands of dollars. For example, if you take out a $150,000, 30-year mortgage at 4.50 percent, multiply 150 by 5.07 (from Table 2-1) to arrive at a $760.50 monthly payment.

Interest Rate	15-Year Mortgage	30-Year Mortgage
4	7.40	4.77
4⅛	7.46	4.85
4¼	7.52	4.92
4⅜	7.59	4.99
4½	7.65	5.07
4⅝	7.71	5.14
4¾	7.78	5.22
4⅞	7.84	5.29
5	7.91	5.37
5⅛	7.98	5.45
5¼	8.04	5.53
5⅜	8.11	5.60
5½	8.18	5.68
5⅝	8.24	5.76
5¾	8.31	5.84
5⅞	8.38	5.92
6	8.44	6.00
6⅛	8.51	6.08
6¼	8.58	6.16
6⅜	8.65	6.24
6½	8.72	6.33
6⅝	8.78	6.41
6¾	8.85	6.49
6⅞	8.92	6.57

Table 2-1: *Monthly Mortgage Payment Calculator*

Use this workspace (reproduced throughout this chapter) to track your estimated homeownership expenses, starting with the mortgage payment:

Item	Estimated Monthly Expense
Mortgage payment	$ _____
Property taxes	+ $ _____
Insurance	+ $ _____
Improvements, maintenance, and other	+ $ _____
Homeownership expenses (pretax)	= $ _____
Tax savings	– $ _____
Homeownership expenses (after-tax benefits)	= $ _____

Property taxes

When you buy and own a home, your local government (typically through what's called a county tax collector's office or an equivalent for your local town) sends you an annual, lump-sum bill for property taxes. Receiving this bill and paying it are never much fun because most communities bill you just once or twice per year. And some homeowners find it aggravating to pay so much in property taxes on top of all the federal and state income and sales taxes they pay. In case you're wondering, property taxes go toward expenses of the local community, such as the public schools and snow plowing.

Should you make a small down payment (typically defined as less than 20 percent of the purchase price), many lenders insist on property tax and insurance *impound accounts.* These accounts require you to pay your property taxes and insurance to the lender each month along with your mortgage payment.

Property taxes are typically based on the value of a property. Although an average property tax rate is about 1.5 to 2.0 percent of the property's purchase price per year, you should understand what the exact rate is in your area. Call the tax collector's office (search online for "Tax Collector," "Treasurer," or "Assessor" and the name of the municipality) in the town where you're contemplating buying a home and ask what the property tax rate is and what additional fees and assessments may apply.

Make sure you compare apples with apples when comparing communities and their property taxes. For example, some communities may nickel-and-dime you for extra assessments for services that are included in the standard property tax bills of other communities.

Real estate listings, which are typically prepared by real estate agents, may list what the current property owner is paying in taxes. But relying on such data to understand what your real estate taxes will be if you buy the property can be financially dangerous. The current owner's taxes may be based on an outdated and much lower property valuation. Just as it's dangerous to drive forward by looking in the rearview mirror of your car, you shouldn't buy a property and budget for property taxes based on the current owner's taxes. Your property taxes (if you buy the home) will be recalculated based on the price you pay for the property.

Item	Estimated Monthly Expense
Mortgage payment	$ _____
Property taxes	+ $ _____
Insurance	+ $ _____
Improvements, maintenance, and other	+ $ _____
Homeownership expenses (pretax)	= $ _____
Tax savings	− $ _____
Homeownership expenses (after-tax benefits)	= $ _____

Insurance

When you purchase a home, your mortgage lender won't allow you to close the purchase until you demonstrate that you have proper homeowners insurance. If you buy the home and make a down payment of, say, 20 percent of the purchase price, the lender is putting up the other 80 percent of the purchase price. So if the home burns to the ground and is a total loss, the lender has more invested financially than you do. In most states, your home is the lender's security for the loan.

Almost all lenders require you to purchase *private mortgage insurance* (PMI) if you put down less than 20 percent of the purchase price when you buy. (We discuss PMI in Chapter 4.)

When you buy a home, you should want to protect your investment in the property (as well as cover the cost of replacing your personal property if it's ever damaged or stolen). In short order, your clothing, furniture, kitchen appliances, and electronics can tally up to a lot of dollars to replace.

 When you purchase homeowners insurance, you should buy the most comprehensive coverage you can and take the highest deductible you can afford to help minimize the cost.

Get quotes on insuring properties as you evaluate them, or ask current owners what they pay for their coverage. (Just remember that some homeowners overpay or don't buy the right kind of protection, so don't take what they pay as gospel.)

_____

_____

_____

If you overlook insurance costs until after you agree to buy a property, you could be in for a rude awakening.

Item	Estimated Monthly Expense
Mortgage payment	$ _____
Property taxes	+ $ _____
Insurance	+ $ _____
Improvements, maintenance, and other	+ $ _____
Homeownership expenses (pretax)	= $ _____
Tax savings	– $ _____
Homeownership expenses (after-tax benefits)	= $ _____

Maintenance and other costs

As a homeowner, you *must* make your mortgage and property tax payments. If you don't, you'll eventually lose your home. Homes also require maintenance over the years. You must do some kinds of maintenance (repairs, for example) at a certain time. You never know precisely when you may need to fix an electrical problem, patch a leaking roof, or replace the washer and dryer — until the problem rears its ugly head, which is why maintenance is difficult to budget for. (Painting and other elective improvements can take place at your discretion.)

As a rule of thumb, expect to spend about 1 percent of your home's purchase price each year on maintenance. So, for example, if you spend $150,000 on a home, you should budget about $1,500 per year (or about $125 per month) for maintenance. Although some years you may spend less, other years you may spend more. When your home's roof goes, for example, replacing it may cost you several years' worth of your budgeted maintenance expenses.

In addition to necessary maintenance, you should be aware (and beware) of what you may spend on nonessential home improvements. This *Other* category can get you into trouble. Advertisements, your neighbors, and your co-workers can all entice you into spending large sums of money on new furniture, endless remodeling projects, landscaping — you name it.

Budget for these nonessentials; otherwise, your home can become a money pit by causing you to spend too much, not save enough, and (possibly) go into debt via credit cards and the like. Unless you're a terrific saver, can easily accomplish your savings goal, and have lots of slack in your budget, be sure not to overlook this part of your homeownership budget.

_____

_____

_____

The amount you expect to spend on improvements is just a guess. It depends on how finished the home is that you buy and on your personal tastes and desires. Consider your previous spending behavior and the types of projects you expect to do as you examine potential homes for purchase.

Item	Estimated Monthly Expense
Mortgage payment	$ _____
Property taxes	+ $ _____
Insurance	+ $ _____
Improvements, maintenance, and other	+ $ _____
Homeownership expenses (pretax)	= $ _____
Tax savings	− $ _____
Homeownership expenses (after-tax benefits)	= $ _____

The tax benefits of homeownership

One of homeownership's benefits is that the IRS and most state governments allow you to deduct, within certain limits, mortgage interest and property taxes when you file your annual income tax return. When you file IRS Form 1040, the mortgage interest and property taxes on your home are itemized deductions on Schedule A. On mortgage loans now taken out, you may deduct the interest on the first $1 million of debt, as well as all the property taxes. The IRS also allows you to deduct the interest costs on a *home equity loan* (second mortgage) to a maximum of $100,000 borrowed.

Just because mortgage interest and property taxes are allowable deductions on your income tax return, don't think that the government is paying for these items for you. Consider that when you earn a dollar of income and must pay income tax on that dollar, you don't pay the entire dollar back to the government in taxes. Your tax bracket (see Table 2-2) determines the amount of taxes you pay on that dollar.

Singles Taxable Income	Married-Filing-Jointly Taxable Income	Federal Tax Rate (Bracket)
$0–$9,325	$0–$18,650	10%
$9,326–$37,950	$18,651–$75,900	15%
$37,951–$91,900	$75,901–$153,100	25%
$91,901–$191,650	$153,101–$233,350	28%
$191,651–$416,700	$233,351–$416,700	33%
$416,701–$418,400	$416,701–$470,700	35%

Table 2-2: *2017 Federal Income Tax Brackets and Rates*

Technically, you pay federal and state taxes, so you should consider your state tax savings as well when calculating your homeownership tax savings. However, to keep things simple and still get a reliable estimate, simply multiply your mortgage payment and property taxes by your *federal* income tax rate. This shortcut works well because the small portion of your mortgage payment that isn't deductible (because it's for the loan repayment) approximately offsets the overlooked state tax savings.

Item	Estimated Monthly Expense
Mortgage payment	$ _____
Property taxes	+ $ _____
Insurance	+ $ _____
Improvements, maintenance, and other	+ $ _____
Homeownership expenses (pretax)	= $ _____
Tax savings	− $ _____
Homeownership expenses (after-tax benefits)	= $ _____

Congratulations! You've totaled what your dream home should cost you on a monthly basis after factoring in the tax benefits of homeownership. Don't forget to plug these expected homeownership costs into your current monthly spending plans to make sure you can afford to spend this much on a home and still accomplish your financial goals.

Closing Costs

On the day when a home becomes yours officially, known as *closing day,* you will pay out more than just the price of the house. Myriad one-time closing costs can leave you poorer or send you running to your relatives for financial assistance.

We don't want you to be unable to close your home purchase or be forced to beg for money from your in-laws. Advance preparation for the closing costs saves your sanity and your finances.

Here are some typical closing costs (listed from those that are usually largest to those that are typically the smallest) and how much to budget for each (exact fees vary by property cost and location).

- **Loan origination fees (points) and other loan charges:** These fees and charges range from nothing to 3 percent of the amount borrowed. Lenders generally charge all sorts of fees for things such as appraising the property, pulling your credit report, preparing loan documents, and processing your application, as well as charging a loan origination fee, which may be 1 or 2 percent of the loan amount. If you're strapped for cash, you can get a loan that has few or no fees; however, such loans have substantially higher interest rates over their lifetimes.

- **Escrow fees:** Escrow fees range from several hundred to over a thousand dollars, based on your home's purchase price. These fees cover the cost of handling all of the purchase-related documents and funds. We explain escrows in more detail in Chapter 8.

- **Homeowners insurance:** This insurance typically costs several hundred to a thousand-plus dollars per year, depending on your home's value and how much coverage you want. As we discuss earlier in this chapter, you can't get a mortgage unless you prove to the lender that you have adequate homeowners insurance coverage. Promising to get this coverage isn't enough; lenders usually insist that you pay the first year's premium on said insurance policy at closing.

- **Title insurance:** This insurance typically costs several hundred to a thousand dollars, depending on the home's purchase price. Lenders require that you purchase title insurance when you buy your home to make sure you have clear, marketable title to the property. Among other things, title insurance protects you and the lender against the remote possibility that the person selling you the home doesn't legally own it.

- **Property taxes:** These taxes typically cost several hundred to a couple thousand dollars and are based on the home's purchase price and the date that escrow closes. At the close of escrow, you may have to reimburse the sellers for any property taxes that they paid in advance. For example, suppose that (before they sell their home to you) the sellers have already paid their property taxes through June 30. If the sale closes on April 30, you owe the sellers two months' property taxes; the tax collector won't refund the property taxes already paid for May and June.

- **Legal fees:** These fees range anywhere from nothing to hundreds of dollars. In some states, lawyers are routinely involved in real estate purchases. In most

states, however, lawyers aren't needed for home purchases as long as the real estate agents use standard,
fill-in-the-blank contracts.

- **Inspections:** Inspection fees can run from $200 to $1,000
(depending on the property's size and the scope of the
inspection). You should never, ever consider buying
a home without inspecting it. Because you're likely
not a home-inspection expert, you benefit from hiring
someone who inspects property as a full-time job (see
Chapter 7). Sometimes you pay these costs directly;
other times you pay these costs at closing.

- **Private mortgage insurance (PMI):** Should you need it,
this insurance can cost you several hundred dollars
annually. As we explain in Chapter 4, if you put less
than 20 percent down on a home, some mortgage
lenders require that you take out private mortgage
insurance. This type of insurance protects the lender
in the event that you default on the loan. At closing,
you need to pay anywhere from a couple months'
premiums to more than a year's premium in advance.
If you can, avoid this cost by making a 20 percent
down payment.

- **Prepaid loan interest:** Lenders charge up to 30 days' interest on your loan to cover the interest that accrues from the date your loan is funded (usually, one business day before the escrow closes) up to 30 days prior to your first regularly scheduled loan payment. How much interest you have to pay depends on the timing of your first loan payment. You can work out this timing with the lender so you don't have to pay any advance loan interest.

- **Recording:** The fee to record the deed and mortgage usually runs about $50.

- **Overnight/courier fees:** These fees usually cost $50 or less. Lenders and other players in real estate deals know snags can occur without warning; because they don't want to derail your transaction or cost themselves money, they often send paperwork the fastest way they can.

- **Notary:** Notary fees run from $10 to $20 *per signature per buyer.* At the close of escrow, you sign all sorts of important documents pledging your worldly possessions should you renege on your mortgage. Therefore, you need to have your signature verified by a notary so everybody in the transaction knows that you are who you say you are.

Closing costs can mount in a hurry. In a typical real estate deal, closing costs total 2 to 5 percent of the property's purchase price. Thus, you shouldn't ignore them in figuring the amount of money you need to close the deal. Having enough to pay the down payment on your loan isn't sufficient.

3

Agents and Brokers

If you're like most people who want to buy or sell a home, you're not an expert on property values, financing, or tax and real estate law. Not understanding what's involved in the process of buying or selling a home can cost you significant sums of money.

How can you find your way through the maze of constantly changing real estate market conditions, local laws, regulations, and tax codes? Where can you sign up for a course in home values? How will you find the time to become an expert in so many fields?

You can't become an expert in all aspects of buying and selling a home, and you don't have to. In this chapter, we explain how to find competent experts who can help you buy or sell a home.

The Team Concept

Smart people sometimes blunder into horrible situations while buying or selling a home. More often than not, what gets them into trouble is ignorance of something that they (or their advisors) should have known but didn't.

Strangely enough, knowing everything yourself isn't important. What is important is having good people on your team — people who know what you need to know so they can help you solve the problems that invariably arise.

You don't have to become an instant expert in home values, mortgages, tax and real estate law, title insurance, and escrows to buy or sell a house. You can hire people who have mastered the skills you lack. After you've assembled a winning team, which you are the leader of, your teammates should give you solid advice so you can make brilliant decisions.

Here's a list of the possible players on your team:

- **You:** You are the most important player on your team. In nearly every home purchase or sale, something goes wrong. You have every right to politely, yet force-fully, insist that things be made right. Remember that you hire (and pay) the players on your team. They work for you.

- **Real estate agent:** Because the home you're about to buy or sell is probably your largest single investment, you must have someone on your team who knows property values. A buyer's agent's primary mission is to help you find your dream home, tell you what the home is worth, and negotiate for it on your behalf. A seller's agent's primary mission is to *accurately* tell you what your house is worth and then negotiate on your behalf to sell it for top dollar.

- **Real estate broker:** Every state issues two kinds of real estate licenses: a salesperson's license and a broker's license. People with broker's licenses must satisfy much tougher educational and experience standards. If your real estate agent isn't an independent broker or the broker for a real estate office, she must be supervised by a broker who is responsible for everything your agent does or fails to do. In a crisis, your transaction's success may depend on backup support from your agent's broker.

- **Lender:** Because most buyers can't pay all cash for their homes, you probably need a loan to buy your dream house. A good lender offers competitively priced loans and may even be able to help you select the best type of loan from the financial minefield of loan programs available today. (See Chapter 5 for details on finding a lender.)

- **Property inspector:** A house's physical condition greatly affects its value. A buyer should have a home he is interested in purchasing thoroughly inspected from roof to foundation to ensure he is getting what he thinks he is buying. (See Chapter 7 for more about inspectors.)

- **Escrow officer:** Mutual distrust is the underlying rule of every real estate deal. The buyer and the seller need a neutral third party, an escrow officer, who handles funds and paperwork related to the transaction without playing favorites. (See Chapter 8 for more about escrow officers.)

- **Financial and tax advisors:** Before you buy a home, you should understand how the purchase or sale fits into the context of your overall financial situation.

- **Lawyer:** You may or may not need a lawyer, depending on your contract's complexity, where the home is located, and your personal comfort level. The purchase agreement you sign when buying or selling a home is a legally binding contract. If you have any questions about your contract's legality, put a lawyer who specializes in real estate law on your team.

Remember that the professionals on your team are *advisors* — not decision makers. You're the boss and decision maker. The buck stops with you.

Beware of experts who offer you gratuitous advice outside their fields of expertise. Good experts don't offer guidance that they aren't qualified to give. If asked, they categorically refuse to give such advice. Instead, they redirect their clients to the proper experts. Good experts are wise enough to know what they don't know and humble enough to admit it. On a more selfish level, they don't want to get sued by their clients for giving lousy advice.

Real Estate Agents

"What's it worth?"

The wrong answer to this question can cost you *big* bucks! Worse yet, there's no simple answer to this deceptively simple question because home prices aren't precise. You can't reduce home prices to a math problem where 2 plus 2 equals 4 now and forevermore. Home prices aren't fixed — on the contrary, they slither all over the place.

Houses sell for *fair market value,* which is whatever buyers offer and sellers accept. Fair market value isn't a specific number; it's a price *range.*

Suppose a buyer makes an offer on a house worth about $250,000. If the seller has a better agent than the buyer does, and the buyer is desperate to buy, the buyer may end up paying $275,000. On the other hand, if the buyer is in no hurry to buy, and her agent is a good negotiator, she may be able to buy the home for $225,000. Home sale prices are often directly related both to the agent's knowledge of what comparable houses have sold for and to the agent's negotiating skills. Of course, other factors (such as the buyer's and seller's motivation, needs, and knowledge) are also important.

A good agent can be the foundation of your real estate team. An agent can help a buyer find a home that meets her needs, negotiate for that home on her behalf, supervise property inspections, and coordinate the closing. Agents often have useful leads for mortgage loans. A good agent's negotiating skills and knowledge of property values can save you thousands of dollars.

In the following sections, we explain how to narrow the field down to good agents who are worthy of their commissions.

Types of agent relationships

Home buyers and sellers can have three different types of relationships with real estate agents. The primary relationships are both types of *single agency*, which is when the agent represents only one of the two parties in the transaction:

- **Seller's agent:** In this form of single agency, the agent works solely for the seller.
- **Buyer's agent:** In this type of single agency, the agent works only for the buyer. A buyer's agent isn't an agent of the seller even if the buyer's agent gets a portion of the commission paid by the seller.

(The third type of relationship you can have with an agent is called *dual agency*, which we don't recommend because it creates a conflict of interest for the agent.)

Buyer's agents still suffer from a conflict of interest inherent in getting a commission that is tied to a percentage of the amount that a buyer spends for a property.

In rare cases, buyer's agents don't accept money from sellers. Instead, a buyer signs a contract to work exclusively with a buyer's agent, and the buyer pays the agent a retainer that is applied toward the fee owed when the buyer's agent finds the buyer a home. Depending on the contract provisions, the retainer may or may not be returned to the buyer if the buyer's agent fails to find the buyer a satisfactory property to purchase.

How agents get paid

Real estate brokerage is an all-or-nothing business. As a rule, agents are paid a commission only when property sells. If the property doesn't sell, agents don't get paid.

This payment method can create a conflict of interest between you and your agent. The payment method won't create a conflict of interest with *good* agents because good agents put your best interests in front of their desire to get paid. You're working with a bad agent, however, if the agent is more interested in quickly closing the sale and having you pay top dollar (if you're the buyer) or accepting a low offer (if you're the seller) than in diligently educating you and getting you the best possible deal.

Here are some answers to common questions about real estate commissions:

- **How much do real estate agents get in commissions?**
  Commissions are calculated as a percentage of the sale price. Depending on local custom, commissions

on homes usually range from 4 to 7 percent of the sale price.

- **Who pays the commission?** Typically, sellers. After all, sellers get money when property sells. Buyers rarely have much money left after making the down payment and paying loan charges, property inspection fees, home-owners insurance premiums, moving costs, and the other expenses of purchase. Because commission is part of the sales price, however, the effective cost of the commission comes out of both the buyer's and seller's pockets.

- **Are commissions negotiable?** Yes. *Listing agreements* (the contracts that property owners sign with brokers to sell property) and purchase agreements usually state that commissions aren't fixed by law and may be nego-tiated between sellers and brokers.

- **How is the commission distributed?** Suppose a house sells for a nice, round $300,000. Assuming a 6 percent commission rate, the sale generates an $18,000 commis-sion. That's a lot of money. At least it would be if it all went to one person, but commissions don't work that way as a rule.

Usually, the commission is divided in half at the close of escrow. The *listing broker*, who represents the sellers, gets half ($9,000, in our example) of the commission, and the other half ($9,000) goes to the *selling broker*, who represents the buyers.

Characteristics of good agents

All good agents have the following characteristics:

- **Good agents educate you.** Your agent knows the home buying and selling process and carefully explains each step so you always understand what's happening. Agents should be patient, not pushy.

- **Good agents don't make decisions for you.** Your agent always explains what your options are so you can make wise decisions regarding your best course of action.

- **Good agents tell you when they think that adding other experts (inspectors, lawyers, and the like) to your team is advisable.** Experts don't threaten a good agent. The agent's ego should always be secondary to the primary mission of serving you well.

_____

_____

_____

- **Good agents voluntarily restrict themselves geographically and by property type.** Your agent has ideally learned that trying to be all things to all people invariably results in mediocre service. Different communities can have radically different market conditions, laws, and restrictions.

- **Good agents are full-time professionals because serving you properly is a full-time job.** To reduce the financial impact of changing jobs, many people begin their real estate careers as part-timers, working as agents after normal business hours and weekends. That's fine for the agents, but not you.

  One of the first questions you must ask any agent you're considering working with is "Are you a full-time agent?" Just as you wouldn't risk letting a part-time lawyer defend you, don't let a part-time agent represent you.

- **Good agents have contacts.** Folks prefer doing business with people they know, respect, and trust. You can use your agent's working relationships with local lenders, property inspectors, lawyers, title officers, insurance agents, government officials, and other real estate agents. Good agents will refer you to highly skilled service providers who offer competitive pricing.

_____

_____

_____

- **Good agents have time.** Agents earn their living selling time, not houses. Success is a two-edged sword for busy agents. An agent who is already working with several other buyers and sellers probably won't have enough surplus time to serve you properly. Occasional scheduling conflicts are unavoidable. But if you often find your needs being neglected because your agent's time is overcommitted, get a new agent.

- **Good agents are technologically savvy.** Good agents know how to use technology to get the job done. They (or their staff) know how to use the Internet to make property searches, can put listing information about your house on a variety of websites, and do online research to keep up with current housing trends. They understand the importance of staying in close touch with you and their other important contacts via cellphone, email, or text messaging.

Selecting your agent

After you know the characteristics of a good agent (see the previous section), you're ready to choose an agent of your very own. We recommend that you interview at least three agents before selecting one.

Finding referral sources

If you have trouble finding three good agents to interview, here are some referral sources:

- **Friends, business associates, and members of religious, professional, and social organizations to which you belong:** In short, anyone you know who's house hunting or who owns a home in your target neighborhood can be a source of agent referrals. If you're selling your house, talk to people who recently sold their house or are in the process of doing so. Don't just ask for names; find out why they liked their agents.

- **Professionals in related fields:** Financial, tax, and legal advisors can be good agent-referral sources.

- **The agent who sold your previous home:** If you're a homeowner who's moving into a new area, ask the agent who sold you your home to recommend a good agent in that area. Good agents network with one another.

- **Sunday open houses:** While you're investigating houses you may want to buy, check out the agents. These agents have already proved (by their open-house activity) that they work the neighborhood in which you want to buy. If you're selling your home, visit houses currently on the market in your neighborhood to see how well the agents hosting the open houses handle the process.

Don't take any referral as gospel. Most people who give referrals have limited or outdated experience with the recommended agent. Furthermore, the person making the referral is probably not a real estate expert.

Requesting an activity list

After you've identified at least three good agents, tell each agent that you plan to interview several agents before you select the one you'll work with.

If you're a seller, start the selection process by inviting these agents to tour your house — individually, of course — so each can prepare a *comparable market analysis* (CMA) for your property. The CMA establishes your house's value by comparing it to other houses in your neighborhood that are approximately the same size, age, and condition as your house.

Whether you're a buyer or a seller, ask each agent to bring to the interview a list of *every* property the agent listed or sold during the preceding 12 months. This list, called the *activity list*, is an extremely powerful analytical tool.

Here's what the activity list should include and how you should use the list during the interview:

- **Property address:** Addresses help you zero in on the agent's geographical focus. See for yourself exactly how many properties the agent sold and listed in your target neighborhood(s). Eliminate agents who are focused outside your area and agents who have no geographical focus.

- **Property type (house, condo, duplex, other):** You can use this information to determine whether the agent works on the kind of property you intend to buy.

- **Sales price:** Does the agent handle property in your price range? An agent who deals in much more or less expensive property than you expect to buy may not be the right agent for you.

- **Days on market (DOM):** Ask agents you interview to specify how long property they listed was on the market before it sold. Compare that to the average DOM for your neighborhood according to statistics developed by a reliable independent source such as the local Multiple Listing Service (MLS). Eliminate agents whose listings take far longer to sell than the average DOM in your area.

- **Date of sale:** Sales activity should be distributed fairly evenly throughout the year. If it isn't, find out why. A lack of recent sales activity may be because of illness or personal problems that may reduce the agent's effectiveness.

- **Whom the agent represented — seller or buyer:** Seasoned agents work about half the time with buyers and the other half with sellers. Newer agents primarily work with buyers. Avoid agents who work primarily with sellers. These agents generally lack either the interest or aptitude to work effectively with buyers.

- **Total dollar value of property sold during the preceding 12 months:** Comparing the three agents' grand-total property sales is a quick way to measure each agent's individual activity and success.

- **Names and current phone numbers of sellers/buyers:** You'll use this later to spot-check references.

_____

_____

_____

Good agents willingly give you their lists and encourage you to check client references. Bad agents don't want you talking to their unhappy clients. Eliminate from consideration any agent who won't give you a comprehensive activity list — she is trying to hide either a lack of sales or unhappy clients.

Interviewing agents

Begin each interview by spending a few minutes analyzing the agent's activity list. After you've finished reviewing the list and had time to organize your thoughts, get answers to the following questions:

- **Are you a full-time agent?** You should have asked this before inviting the agent to be interviewed. If you forgot, do it now. Don't work with part-time agents.

- **Whom do you represent?** This topic gets back to the fundamental question of agency. Is the agent representing you exclusively, or is he a dual agent who represents both you and the seller? Be sure you know exactly whom your agent represents at all times.

- **What can you tell me about your office?** Discuss office size, staff support, market specialization, and reputation. See whether the agent's broker is knowledgeable, is available to you if necessary, and is a good problem-solver. In a crunch, your transaction's success (or failure) may depend on the quality of backup support that you and the agent receive.

- **How long have you been an agent?** You want an agent who keeps learning and growing. After five years in real estate, a good agent has five years' experience, whereas a mediocre agent has one year's experience five times. Time is, by itself, no guarantee of competence.

- **Do you have a salesperson's license or a broker's license?** An agent must satisfy more rigorous educational and field sales experience requirements to get a broker's license. Many fine agents have only a salesperson's license throughout their entire careers. Although a broker's license isn't a guarantee of excellence, good agents often obtain a broker's license to improve their professional skills and to give themselves an advantage in agent-selection situations.

- **Do you hold any professional designations? Have you taken any real estate classes recently? What do you**

read to keep current in your field? Taking continuing-education courses and reading to stay abreast of changes in real estate brokerage are good signs. So is obtaining professional designations.

- **What is your understanding of my home buying needs?** You've probably already told the agent what type of property you want to buy, the neighborhood you want to live in, and how much you can spend. See whether the agent remembers what you said. If the agent doesn't remember, watch out. You need an agent who listens carefully to what you say.

- **What do you think of the other two agents (name them) whom I'm interviewing?** To encourage frankness, assure the agents that you won't repeat what they say to you. Good agents don't build themselves up by tearing down other agents. If all three agents are good ones, you won't hear any derogatory comments. However, if one of the agents (or the agent's firm) has a bad reputation in the real estate community, the other two agents should tell you.

- **How many other buyers and sellers are you currently representing?** If, for example, the agent holds three listings open every weekend and is working with six other buyers, where do you fit in? Although some scheduling conflicts are inevitable, you shouldn't have to contort your life to fit the agent's schedule. A good agent has time to accommodate your schedule.

- **Do you work in partnership with another agent or use assistants?** Some agents team up with another agent to handle buyers and sellers jointly. If this is the case, you must interview both agents. Other agents delegate time-consuming detail work to their assistants so they can focus on critical points in the transaction. If an agent relies on such assistants, be sure that the assistants are qualified and that you understand exactly how and when during the process the agent will work directly with you.

- **Is there anything I haven't asked about you or your firm that you think I should know?** Perhaps the agent is planning to change firms or is leaving next week to take an 80-day trip around the world. Maybe the agent's broker is going out of business. *This is the make-sure-I-find-out-everything-I-need-to-know-to-make-a-good-decision question.*

_____

_____

_____

Checking agents' references

Here's your chance to profit from other people's mistakes, which is infinitely preferable to goofing up yourself. You should have activity lists with the names and phone numbers of every buyer and seller that the agents represented during the past 12 months. You can pick and choose the people you want to call instead of being restricted to a highly selective list of references who think that these agents are the best in town.

You don't have to call each and every client to check references. You can get an accurate picture of the agents by making as few as six calls per agent.

Here's a fast, easy way to get a representative sampling of client references:

1. **If you're a buyer, ignore all references from sellers. If you're a seller, ignore all references from buyers.**

   Doing so probably slices the list in half.

2. **Zero in on people who bought (or sold) property similar in price, location, and property type to what you want to buy (or sell).**

3. **Call two of those representative buyers (or sellers) who purchased (or sold) a home about 12 months ago, another two buyers (or sellers) who bought (or sold) 6 months ago, and two buyers (or sellers) whose escrows closed most recently.**

   By spreading references over the past year, you can find out whether the agent's level of service has been consistently good.

Now that you've identified which people to call, here's what to ask when you have them on the phone:

- **Is the agent trustworthy? Honest? Did the agent follow through on promises?** Your agent can't be even the tiniest bit untrustworthy, dishonest, or unreliable. A negative answer to any of these questions is the kiss of death.

- **Did the agent have enough time to serve you properly? Was the agent available as required to fit your schedule?** Occasional scheduling conflicts are okay. Frequent conflicts are unacceptable.

- **Did the agent explain everything that happened during the buying or selling process clearly and in**

sufficient detail to satisfy you? What one person thinks is sufficient detail may not be nearly enough information for another. You know which type of person you are — question agent references accordingly.

- **Did the agent set realistic contract deadlines and meet or beat them?** "Time is of the essence" is a condition of every real estate contract. Contract time frames for obtaining a loan, completing property inspections, and the like are extremely important and must be strictly adhered to, or the deal falls apart. Good agents prepare well-written contracts with realistic time frames and then ensure that all deadlines are met.

- **Do the words self-starter, committed, and motivated describe the agent?** No one likes pushy people. But if you're under pressure to buy quickly, the last thing you want is a lethargic agent. Find out how energetically the agent in question is prepared to work.

- **Who found the home you bought — you or the agent?** This question is a double-check of the agent's market knowledge. Good agents know not only what's already on the market but also which houses will be coming on the market soon. You shouldn't have to find the house you buy — that's your agent's job.

- **Did the agent negotiate a good price for your home?** See whether the agent's buyers still think they got a good deal. Good agents are frugal when spending their clients' money. Good agents use their knowledge of property values and their negotiating skills to make sure their buyers pay the fair market value or less for the homes they buy. People who bought homes six months or a year ago can tell you how well their purchase prices have stood the test of time.

- **Would you use the agent again?** This is the ultimate test of customer satisfaction. If someone says "no," find out why not. The negative answer may be due to a personality conflict between the client and the agent that won't bother you. On the other hand, the negative answer may reveal a horrendous flaw that you haven't yet discovered.

- **Is there anything I haven't asked you about the agent or the agent's office that you think I should know?** You never know what you'll find out when you ask the famous catchall question.

_____

_____

_____

Making your decision

After analyzing all three agents' sales activity, interviewing the agents, and talking to their clients, you have most of the facts you need to make an informed decision. Here are three final considerations to help you select the paragon of virtue that you need on your real estate team:

- **Will you be proud having the agent represent you?** People who deal with your agent will form opinions of you based on their impressions of your agent. You can't afford to have anyone on your team who isn't a highly skilled professional.

- **Do you communicate well with the agent?** Good agents make sure you understand everything they say. If you can't understand your agent, don't blame yourself; the agent is a poor communicator.

- **Do you enjoy the agent's personality?** Home buying or selling is stressful. You'll be sharing some extremely intense situations with your agent. Working with an agent you like may transform the process from a horrible experience into an exciting adventure — or at least a tolerable transaction.

Brokers

Selecting a broker is easy. When you choose an agent, your agent's broker goes along for the ride. It's a package deal.

If your transaction rolls merrily along from the time your offer is accepted to the close of escrow, you probably never meet the broker. But if a truly nasty problem arises, you can turn to the broker to work through the issues.

All states issue two markedly different types of real estate licenses: one for salespeople (agents) and one for brokers. Agents who have broker's licenses must satisfy much more stringent educational and experience standards than agents with a salesperson's license do.

Your agent may have either type of license. Broker licensees have the option either to operate independently or to work for another broker. An agent who has a salesperson's license, on the other hand, *must* work under a broker's direct supervision so you have access to the broker's higher level of expertise should you need it.

Here are some characteristics of good brokers:

- **Excellent reputation:** The broker's image, good or bad, will be obvious from comments that you hear while checking agent references. You want everyone involved in your transaction working with you because of your broker's reputation, not in spite of it. Buying or selling a home is hard enough without the added burden of having to overcome guilt by association. If an agent's references disparage the agent's broker, dump the agent.

- **Extensive business relationships:** Good brokers develop and maintain relationships with the people whom their office deals with — other brokers, lenders, title officers, city officials, and the like. Brokers with strong business relationships can work near-miracles for you in a crisis.

- **Strong problem-solving skills:** Participants in real estate transactions sometimes get highly emotional. When your life savings are on the line, you may occasionally lash out at your agent and the other players. Someone has to resolve the resulting quarrels and misunderstandings. That someone is the broker.

The broker's job is to help solve your problems. Call your broker into the game if your agent is stymied by a tough problem or if you're having trouble with your agent. Everything your agent does or fails to do is ultimately the broker's responsibility.

4

Down Payments

We don't want you to be surprised when you finally set out to purchase a home. That's why now, in the comfort of your rental, we'd like you to consider the following:

- How much money you should save for the down payment and closing costs for the purchase of your home
- Where your down-payment money is going to come from
- How you should invest this money while you're awaiting the purchase and closing

The 20 Percent Solution

Ideally, when buying a home you should have enough money accumulated for a down payment of 20 percent of the property's purchase price. Why 20 percent and not 10 or 15 or 25 or 30 percent? Twenty percent down is the magic number because it's generally a big enough cushion to protect lenders from default. Suppose, for example, that a buyer puts only 10 percent down, property values drop 5 percent, and the buyer defaults on the loan. When the lender forecloses — *after* paying a real estate commission, transfer tax, and other expenses of sale — the lender will be in the hole. Lenders don't like losing money. They've found that they're far less likely to lose money on mortgages where the borrower has put up a down payment of at least 20 percent of the property's value.

If, like most people, you plan to borrow money from a bank or other mortgage lender, be aware that almost all require you to obtain (and pay for) private mortgage insurance (PMI) if your down payment is less than 20 percent of the property's purchase price. Although PMI typically adds several hundred dollars annually to your loan's cost, it protects the lender financially if you default. (When you make a down payment of less than 20 percent, you can also expect worse loan terms, such as higher up-front fees and/or a higher ongoing interest rate on a mortgage.)

PMI isn't a permanent cost. Your need for PMI vanishes when you can prove that you have at least 20 percent *equity* (home value minus loan balance outstanding) in the property. The 20 percent can come from loan paydown, appreciation, improvements that enhance the property's value, or any combination thereof. Also note that to remove PMI, most mortgage lenders require that an appraisal be done — at your expense.

Ways to Buy with Less Money Down

If you're just starting to save or are still paying off student loans or digging out from consumer debt, saving 20 percent of a property's purchase price as a down payment plus closing costs can seem like a financial mountain.

Don't panic, and don't give up. Here's a list of time-tested ways to overcome this seemingly gargantuan obstacle:

- **Boost your savings rate.** Say that you want to accumulate $30,000 for your home purchase, and you're saving just $100 per month. At this rate, it will take you nearly two decades to reach your savings goal! However, if you can boost your savings rate by $300 per month, you should reach your goal in about five years.

  Being efficient with your spending is always a good financial habit, but saving faster is a *necessity* for nearly all prospective home buyers. Without benevolent relatives or other sources for a financial windfall, you're going to need to accumulate money the old-fashioned way that millions of other home buyers have done in the past: by gradually saving it.

- **Set your sights lower.** Twenty percent of a big number is a big number, so it stands to reason that 20 percent of a smaller number is a smaller number. If the down payment and closing costs needed to purchase a $300,000 home are stretching you, scale back to a $240,000 or $200,000 home, which should slash your required cash for the home purchase by about 20 to 33 percent.

- **Check out low-down-payment loan programs.** Some lenders offer low-down-payment mortgage programs where you can put down, say, 10 percent of the purchase price. To qualify for such programs, you generally must have excellent credit, have two to three months' worth of reserves for your housing expenses, and purchase private mortgage insurance (PMI). In addition to the extra expense of PMI, expect to get worse loan terms — higher interest rates and more up-front fees — with such low-money-down loans. Check with local lenders and real estate agents in your area. The best low down-payment loan is the FHA purchase program. If you are a veteran, get a VA loan.

  Unless you're champing at the bit to purchase a home, take more time and try to accumulate a larger down payment. However, if you're the type of person who has trouble saving and may never save a 20 percent down payment, buying with less money down may be your best option. In this situation, be sure to shop around for the best loan terms.

- **Access retirement accounts.** Some employers allow you to borrow against your retirement savings plan. Just be sure you understand the repayment rules so you don't get tripped up and forced to treat the withdrawal as a taxable distribution. You're allowed to make penalty-free withdrawals from Individual Retirement Accounts for a first-time home purchase.

- **Get family help.** Your parents or grandparents may like to help you with the down payment and closing costs for your dream home. Why would they do that? Well, perhaps they had financial assistance from family when they bought a home way back when. Another possibility is that they have more money accumulated for their future and retirement than they may need. If they have substantial assets, holding onto all of those assets until their death could trigger estate taxes.

  If a family member broaches the topic of giving or lending you money for a home purchase, go ahead and discuss the matter. But in many situations, you (as the prospective home buyer) may need to raise the issue first. Some parents aren't comfortable bringing up the topic of money or may be worried that you'll take their offer in the wrong way.

Where to Invest the Down Payment

 As with all informed investing decisions, which investment(s) you consider for money earmarked for your down payment should be determined by how soon you need the money. The longer the time frame during which you can invest, the more growth-oriented and riskier (that is, more *volatile*) an investment you may consider. Conversely, when you have a short time frame — five years or less — during which you can invest, choosing volatile investments is dangerous.

When the stock market is rising, some folks are tempted to keep down-payment money in stocks. After all, when you're getting returns of 20 percent or more annually, you'll reach your down-payment savings goal far more quickly.

Investing down-payment money in stocks is a dangerous strategy. Your expected home purchase may be delayed for years due to a sinking investment portfolio. Stocks are a generally inappropriate investment for down-payment money you expect to tap within the next five years. More aggressive individual stocks should have an even longer time horizon — ideally, seven to ten or more years.

Investments for five years or less

Most prospective home buyers aren't in a position to take many risks with their down-payment money. The sooner you expect to buy, the less risk you should take. Unless you don't expect to buy for at least five years, you shouldn't consider investing in more growth-oriented investments, such as stocks.

Although it may appear boring, the first (and likely best) place for accumulating your down-payment money is in a money market mutual fund. As with bank savings accounts, money market mutual funds don't put your principal at risk — the value of your original investment *(principal)* doesn't fluctuate. Rather, you simply earn interest on the money that you've invested. Money market funds invest in supersafe investments, such as Treasury bills, bank certificates of deposit, and *commercial paper* (short-term IOUs issued by the most creditworthy corporations).

If you really want to save through a bank, shop around. Smaller savings and loans and credit unions tend to offer more competitive yields than do the larger banks that spend significantly on advertising and have branches on nearly every corner. Remember, more overhead means lower yields for your money.

In addition to higher yields, the best money market funds offer check writing (so you can easily access your money) and come in tax-free versions. The better money market funds also offer telephone exchange and redemption and automated, electronic exchange services with your bank account. Automatic investment comes in handy for accumulating your down payment for a home purchase. Once per month, for example, you can have money transferred from your bank account into your money market fund.

Because a particular type of money market fund (general, Treasury, or tax-free municipal) is basically investing in the same securities as its competitors, opt for a fund that keeps lean-and-mean expenses. A money fund's operating expenses, which are deducted before payment of dividends, are the major factor in determining its yield. As with the high overhead of bank branches, the higher a money fund's operating expenses, the lower its yield. We recommend good ones in this section.

When you're not in a high federal tax bracket, and you're not in a high state tax bracket (that is, you pay less than 5 percent in state taxes), consider the following taxable money market funds for your home down-payment money:

- Fidelity Cash Reserves ($2,500 to open)

- T. Rowe Price Summit Cash Reserves ($25,000 to open)

- Vanguard's Prime Money Market ($3,000 to open)

You can invest in a money market fund that invests in U.S. Treasury money market funds, which have the backing of the U.S. federal government! From a tax standpoint, because U.S. Treasuries are state-tax-free but federally taxable, U.S. Treasury money market funds are appropriate when you're not in a high federal tax bracket but you are in a high state tax bracket (5 percent or higher). Should you choose to invest in a money market fund that invests in the U.S. Treasury, consider these:

- Fidelity's Government Money Market ($2,500 to open)

- USAA's Treasury Money Market ($3,000 to open)

- Vanguard Federal Money Market ($3,000 to open)

Municipal (also known as *muni*) money market funds invest in short-term debt (meaning that it matures within the next few years) issued by state and local governments. A municipal money market fund, which pays you federally tax-free dividends, invests in munis issued by state and local governments throughout the country. A state-specific municipal fund invests in state and local government-issued munis for one state, such as New York. So if you live in New York and buy a New York municipal fund, the dividends on that fund are generally free of both federal and New York state taxes.

How do you decide whether to buy a nationwide or state-specific municipal money market fund? Federal-tax-free-only money market funds are appropriate when you're in a high federal tax bracket but not a high state tax bracket (less than 5 percent). Your state may not have good (or any) state-tax-free money market funds available. If you live in any of those states, you're likely best off with one of the following national money market funds:

- T. Rowe Price Summit Municipal Money Market ($25,000 to open)

- USAA Tax-Exempt Money Market ($3,000 to open)

- Vanguard Tax-Exempt Money Market ($3,000 to open)

Investments for more than five years

Should you expect to hold onto your home down-payment money for more than five years, you can comfortably consider riskier investments, such as longer-term bonds, as well as more conservative stocks. Eric covers these investments in his book *Back to Basics: Investing* (Wiley).

_____

_____

_____

5

Mortgages

Most people need to take out a mortgage to buy a home for the simple reason that doing so is the only way we can afford a home that meets our needs. This chapter helps you comprehend mortgages and then choose one.

Mortgage Basics

A *mortgage* is nothing more than a loan you obtain to close the gap between the cash you have for a down payment and the purchase price of the home you're buying. Homes in your area may cost $170,000, $470,000, or more. No matter — most people don't have that kind of spare cash in their piggy banks.

Mortgages require that you make monthly payments to repay your debt. The mortgage payments comprise *interest*, which is what the lender charges for use of the money you borrow, and *principal*, which is repayment of the original amount you borrow.

As noted in Chapter 2, the lender may also insist that you establish an *impound account* if your down payment is less than 20 percent of the purchase price. Impound accounts require that you pay your monthly property taxes and insurance to the lender with your mortgage payment. Your lender puts impound account funds into a special escrow, and then makes these payments on your behalf when they're due. Escrows are covered in detail in Chapter 8.

Figuring out how to select a mortgage to meet your needs ensures that you'll be a happy homeowner for years to come. You also need to understand how to get a good deal when shopping around for a mortgage because your mortgage is typically the biggest monthly expense of homeownership. Paying more in total interest charges over the life of your mortgage than you originally pay for your home itself isn't unusual.

Suppose you borrow $144,000 (and contribute $36,000 from your savings as a 20 percent down payment) for the purchase of your $180,000 home. If you borrow that $144,000 with a

30-year, fixed-rate mortgage at 7 percent, you end up paying a whopping $200,892 in interest charges alone over the life of your loan. That $200,892 is not only a great deal of interest; it's also more than the home's purchase price or the loan amount you originally borrowed!

So you don't spend any more than you need to on your mortgage, and so you get the mortgage that best meets your needs, the time has come to understand the mortgage options available to you.

Fixed versus Adjustable

Many different mortgage options are available for your choosing. The variations can be significant or trivial, expensive or less costly.

Two fundamentally different types of mortgages exist: fixed-rate mortgages and adjustable-rate mortgages. The chief differences between these two main types of mortgages are how their interest rate is determined and whether it can change.

Distinguishing fixed-rate mortgages from adjustables

Before adjustable-rate mortgages came into being, only fixed-rate mortgages existed. Usually issued for 15- or 30-year periods, *fixed-rate mortgages* have interest rates that are *fixed* (unchanging) during the entire life of the loan.

With a fixed-rate mortgage, the interest rate stays the same, and your monthly mortgage payment amount never changes. No surprises, no uncertainty, and no anxiety for you over interest-rate changes and changes in your monthly payment.

On the other hand, *adjustable-rate mortgages* (ARMs for short) have an interest rate that varies (or *adjusts*). The interest rate on an ARM typically adjusts every 6 to 12 months, but it may change as frequently as every month.

The interest rate on an ARM is primarily determined by what's happening overall to interest rates. When interest rates are generally on the rise, odds are that your ARM will experience increasing rates, thus increasing the size of your mortgage payment. Conversely, when interest rates fall, ARM interest rates and payments generally fall.

If you like change, you may think that adjustable-rate mortgages sound good. Please read on, because even if you believe that variety is the spice of life, you may not like the financial variety of adjustables.

Making the fixed/adjustable decision

So how do you choose whether to take a fixed-rate or an adjustable-rate loan?

In this section, we talk you through the pros and cons of your mortgage options, but as we do, please keep one important fact in mind: In the final analysis, the mortgage that's best for you hinges on your personal and financial situation now and in the future. *You* are the one who's best positioned to make the call as to whether a fixed or an adjustable loan better matches your situation and desires.

Fixed-rate mortgages

It stands to reason that because the interest rate doesn't vary with a fixed-rate mortgage, the advantage of this type of mortgage is that you always know what your monthly payment is going to be. Thus, budgeting and planning are easier.

You'll pay a premium, in the form of a higher interest rate (generally ½ to ¾ percent), to get a lender to commit to lending you money over many years at a fixed rate. The longer the mortgage lender agrees to accept a fixed interest rate, the more risk that lender is taking. A lender who agrees to loan you money, for example, over 30 years at 6 percent will be weeping if interest rates skyrocket to the 15-plus percent level.

In addition to paying a premium interest rate when you take out the loan, another potential drawback to fixed-rate loans is that if interest rates fall significantly after you take out your mortgage, you face the risk of being stranded with your costly mortgage. That could happen if (because of deterioration in your financial situation or a decline in your property's value) you don't qualify to *refinance* (get a new loan to replace the old one). Even if you do qualify to refinance, doing so takes time and usually costs money for a new appraisal, loan fees, and title insurance. This may be 2 to 3 percent or more of the loan amount. A $200,000 loan, for example, might cost $4,000 to $6,000 or more to refinance.

Adjustable-rate mortgages

Fixed-rate mortgages aren't your only option. Mortgage lenders were intelligent enough to realize that they couldn't foresee how much future interest rates would rise or fall; thus, adjustable-rate mortgages (*adjustables* or ARMs for short) were born.

Although some adjustables are more volatile than others, all are similar in that they *fluctuate* (or float) with the market level of interest rates. If the interest rate fluctuates, so does your monthly payment. And therein lies the risk: Because a mortgage payment is likely to be a big monthly expense for you, an adjustable-rate mortgage that's adjusting upward may wreak havoc with your budget.

You may ask, "Why would anyone choose an adjustable-rate mortgage?" Well, people who are stretching themselves — such as some first-time buyers or those *trading up* to a more expensive home — may financially force themselves into accepting adjustable-rate mortgages. Because an ARM starts out at a lower interest rate, such a mortgage enables you to *qualify* to borrow more. As we discuss in Chapter 2, just because you can qualify to borrow more doesn't mean you can *afford* to borrow that much, given your other financial goals and needs.

Some home buyers who can qualify for either an adjustable-rate or a fixed-rate mortgage of the same size have a choice and choose the fluctuating adjustable-rate mortgage. Why? Because they may very well save themselves money, in the form of smaller total interest charges, with an adjustable-rate loan rather than a fixed-rate loan.

_____

_____

_____

Because you accept the risk of a possible increase in interest rates, mortgage lenders cut you a little slack. The *initial interest rate* (also sometimes referred to as the *teaser rate*) on an adjustable should be less than the initial interest rate on a comparable fixed-rate loan. In fact, an ARM's interest rate for the first year or two of the loan is generally lower than the rate on a fixed-rate mortgage.

Another situation when adjustable-rate loans have an advantage over fixed-rate mortgages is when interest rates decline and you don't qualify to refinance your mortgage to reap the advantage of lower rates. The good news for homeowners who are unable to refinance and who have an ARM is that they usually capture many of the benefits of the lower rates. With a fixed-rate loan, you must refinance to realize the benefits of a decline in interest rates.

The downside to an adjustable-rate loan is that if interest rates in general rise, your loan's interest and monthly payment will likely rise, too. During most time periods, if rates rise more than 1 or 2 percent and stay elevated, the adjustable-rate loan is likely to cost you more than a fixed-rate loan.

Before you make the final choice between a fixed-rate mortgage and an adjustable-rate mortgage, read the following two sections.

What would rising interest rates do to your finances?

Far too many home buyers take out an adjustable-rate mortgage because doing so allows them to stretch and borrow more to buy a more expensive home. Overborrowing is sometimes encouraged by real estate and mortgage salespeople. After all, these salespeople's income, in the form of a commission, is a function of the cost of the home you buy and the size of the mortgage you take on. Resist the temptation to overspend. Buy what you can afford.

When considering an ARM, you must understand what rising interest rates (and, therefore, a rising monthly mortgage payment) would do to your personal finances. Consider taking an ARM only if you can answer all the following questions in the affirmative:

- Is your monthly budget such that you can afford higher mortgage payments and still accomplish other financial goals that are important to you, such as saving for retirement?

- Do you have an emergency reserve (equal to at least six months of living expenses) that you can tap into to make the potentially higher monthly mortgage payments?

_____

_____

_____

- Can you afford the highest payment allowed on the adjustable-rate mortgage?

  The mortgage lender can tell you the highest possible monthly payment, which is the payment you would owe if the interest rate on your ARM went to the lifetime interest-rate cap allowed on the loan.

- If you're stretching to borrow near the maximum the lender allows or an amount that will test the limits of your budget, are your job and income stable? If you're depending on financial help from your spouse, is your spouse's job and income secure?

- If you expect to have children in the future, have you considered that your household expenses will rise and your income may fall with their arrival?

- Can you handle the psychological stress of changing interest rates and mortgage payments?

If you're fiscally positioned to take on the financial risks inherent to an adjustable-rate mortgage, by all means consider taking one. The odds are with you to save money, in the form of lower interest charges and payments, with an ARM. Your interest rate starts lower (and generally stays lower, if the overall level of interest rates doesn't change). Even if rates do go up, as they sometimes do, they'll surely come back down. So if you can stick with your ARM through times of high and low interest rates, you should still come out ahead.

Also recognize that although ARMs do carry the risk of a fluctuating interest rate, almost all adjustable-rate loans limit, or *cap*, the rise in the interest rate allowed on your loan. We wouldn't recommend that you take an ARM without caps. Typical caps are 2 percent per year and 6 percent over the life of the loan.

Consider an adjustable-rate mortgage only if you're financially and emotionally secure enough to handle the maximum possible payments over an extended period of time. ARMs work best for borrowers who take out smaller loans than they're qualified for or who consistently save more than 10 percent of their monthly income. If you do choose an ARM, make sure you have a significant cash cushion that's accessible in the event that rates go up. Don't take an adjustable just because the initially lower interest rate allows you to afford a more expensive home. Better to buy a home that you can afford with a fixed-rate mortgage.

How long do you expect to stay in the home or hold the mortgage?

This is the single most important question you need to answer. As we explain earlier in this chapter, a mortgage lender takes more risk when lending money at a fixed rate of interest for many (15 to 30) years. Lenders charge you a premium, in the form of a higher interest rate than what the ARM starts at, for the interest-rate risk that they assume with a fixed-rate loan.

If you don't plan or expect to stay in your home for a long time, consider an ARM. Saving money on interest charges for most adjustables is usually guaranteed in the first two to three years because an ARM starts at a lower interest rate than a fixed-rate loan does. If you're reasonably certain that you'll hold onto your home for fewer than five years, you should come out ahead with an adjustable. However, you should also ask yourself why you're going to all the trouble and expense of buying a home that you expect to sell so soon.

If you expect to hold onto your home and mortgage for a long time — more than five years — a fixed-rate loan may make more sense, especially when you're not in a position to withstand the fluctuating monthly payments that come with an ARM.

If you're on the fence, go with the fixed-rate loan. A fixed-rate loan is financially safer than an ARM.

Deciding on your loan's life: 15 years or 30?

After you decide which type of mortgage — fixed or adjustable — you want, you may think that your mortgage quandaries are behind you. Unfortunately, they're not. You also need to make another important choice — between a 15-year and a 30-year mortgage.

When you're stretching to buy the home you want, you may need to take the longer-term, 30-year mortgage. Doing so isn't necessarily bad and, in fact, has advantages.

The main advantage that a 30-year mortgage has over its 15-year peer is that it has lower monthly payments that free up more of your monthly income for other purposes, including saving for other important financial goals (such as retirement). A 30-year mortgage has lower monthly payments because you have a longer period to repay it (which translates into more payments). A fixed-rate, 30-year mortgage with an interest rate of 7 percent, for example, has payments that are approximately 25 percent lower than those on a comparable 15-year mortgage.

_____

_____

_____

What if you can afford the higher payments that a 15-year mortgage requires? You shouldn't necessarily take it. What if, instead of making large payments on the 15-year mortgage, you make smaller payments on a 30-year mortgage and put that extra money to productive use?

If you do, indeed, make productive use of that extra money, the 30-year mortgage may be for you. A terrific potential use for that extra dough is to contribute it to a tax-deductible retirement account that you have access to. Contributions that you add to employer-based 401(k) and 403(b) plans (and self-employed SEP-IRAs) not only give you an immediate reduction in taxes but also enable your investment to compound, tax-deferred, over the years ahead.

If you exhaust your options for contributing to all the retirement accounts that you can, and if you find it challenging to save money anyway, the 15-year mortgage may offer you a good forced-savings program.

When you elect to take a 30-year mortgage, you retain the flexibility to pay it off faster if you so choose. Constraining yourself with the 15-year mortgage's higher monthly payments does carry a risk. Should you fall on tough financial times, you may not be able to meet the required mortgage payments.

Finding a Lender

Unless you enjoy throwing away thousands of dollars, you need to shop around for the best deal on a mortgage. Whether you do the legwork on your own or hire someone to help you doesn't matter. But you must make sure that this comparison shopping gets done.

Suppose you're in the market for a 30-year, $100,000 mortgage. If, through persistent and wise shopping, you're able to obtain a mortgage that is, for example, 0.5 percent per year lower in interest charges than you otherwise would have gotten, you'll save about $11,000 over the life of the loan. You can double those savings for a $200,000 mortgage.

Although we encourage you to find the lowest-cost lenders, we must first issue a caution: Should someone offer you a deal that's much better than any other lender's, be skeptical. Such a lender may be baiting you with a loan that doesn't exist or with one for which you can't qualify, and then you'll get stuck with a higher-cost loan if you don't have time to apply for another mortgage elsewhere.

Shopping on your own

Most areas have no shortage of mortgage lenders. Although having a large number of options to choose from is good for competition, so many alternatives can also make shopping a headache.

Many different types of companies offer mortgages today. The most common mortgage *originators* are banks, savings and loan associations, and mortgage bankers.

Mortgage bankers do only mortgages, and the best ones offer competitive interest rates on a broad selection of mortgage programs, including FHA, Fannie Mae, Freddie Mac, and VA, as well as state and local Housing Agency loans. Mortgage bankers can also be flexible and competitive with loan fees.

Smaller banks and savings and loans can have good deals as well. Big banks usually don't offer the best interest rates and only allow you to choose from their bank's loan programs.

As you begin your mortgage safari, you don't have to go it alone. If you've done a good job selecting a real estate agent to help you with your home purchase, the agent should be able to give you a short list of good lenders and mortgage brokers (see the following section) in the area. Just remember to compare these lenders' loans and rates with those of some other mortgage lenders that you find on your own.

The Internet offers yet another method for tapping into companies in a particular line of work. Family, friends, and co-workers are also good sources of referrals, especially if their loan experience is recent.

Working with a mortgage broker

Mortgage brokers are middlemen, independent of banks or other financial institutions that have money to lend. They can do the mortgage shopping for you. But first get a list of their five most recent clients so you can do a reference check.

If your credit history and ability to qualify for a mortgage are questionable, a good licensed mortgage broker can help polish and package your application and steer you to the few lenders that may make you a loan.

Mortgage brokers typically tell you that they can get you the best loan deal by shopping among many lenders. They may further argue that another benefit of using their service is that they can explain the multitude of loan choices, help you select a loan, and assist with the morass of paperwork that's required to get a loan.

Good mortgage brokers can deliver on most of these promises, and for this service, they receive a cut of the amount that you borrow — typically, 0.5 to as much as 2 percent on smaller loans.

If you're going to work with a mortgage broker, keep in mind that such brokers are in the business of "selling" mortgages and derive a commission from this work, just as do salespeople who sell cars. A difference, though, is that the interest rate and fees that you pay to get most mortgages through a broker are the same as what you would pay a lender directly. Lenders reason that they can afford to share their normal fees with an outside mortgage broker who isn't employed by the bank. After all, if you got the loan directly from the bank, you'd have to work with and take up more of the time of one of the bank's mortgage employees.

The commission that the mortgage broker receives from the lender isn't set in stone and is completely negotiable, especially on larger loans. On a $100,000 loan, a 1 percent commission amounts to $1,000. The same commission rate on a $300,000 loan results in a $3,000 cut for the broker, even though this three-times-larger loan doesn't take up three times as much of the mortgage broker's time. You have every right to inquire of the mortgage broker what his take is. Don't be embarrassed;

_____

_____

_____

it's your money, and you have every right to know this information! Ask — and don't hesitate to negotiate.

> Be sure to get all costs and fees in writing before committing to take a loan. Always ask if the mortgage broker is receiving a *yield spread premium* from the lender. This is an undisclosed fee that you pay for with a higher interest rate on your loan. The Federal Good Faith Estimates Law requires that you receive this detailed estimate within three days after the mortgage broker gets your loan application. Be sure to read it. Ask questions if there's anything in the estimate that you don't understand. The estimate isn't carved in stone — it's negotiable.

In addition to understanding and negotiating a commission with the mortgage broker, get answers to the following questions when choosing a mortgage broker:

- **How many lenders does the broker do business with, and how does the broker keep up to date with new lenders and loans that may be better?** Some mortgage brokers, out of habit, send all of their business to just a few lenders and don't get you the best deals. Ask brokers which lenders have approved the broker to represent them.

- **How knowledgeable is the broker about the loan programs, and does the broker have the patience to explain all of a loan's important features?** The more lenders a mortgage broker represents, the less likely the broker is to know the nuances of each and every loan. Be especially wary of a salesperson who aggressively pushes certain loan programs.

If you're on the fence about using a mortgage broker, take this simple test: If you're the type of person who dreads shopping and waits until the last minute to buy a gift, a good mortgage broker can probably help and save you money. A competent mortgage broker can be of greatest value to those who don't bother shopping around for a good deal or who may be shunned by most lenders.

6

Negotiating

When you're buying or selling a house, generally everything from the purchase price to the date that escrow closes is negotiable. Given today's high home prices in most of the densely populated parts of the United States, buying a home is the ultimate in high-stakes negotiating. Good negotiators come out of a home purchase smiling. Bad negotiators take it in the wallet.

This chapter explains the basic rules and process for negotiating for buyers and sellers.

Basic Rules of Negotiating

If you take the right steps, you end up in the right place. Your deal can practically take care of itself if you follow these basic negotiating guidelines:

- **Conduct all negotiations face to face.** Never let your agent or lawyer "save time" by using the phone to negotiate important issues. It's too easy for people to say "no" over the phone. Even if the other party agrees with everything you want during a phone conversation, they may change their minds when it's time to sign on the dotted line.

- **Get everything in writing.** Written contracts exist because people have lousy memories. If you want your deal to be enforceable in a court of law, put all the terms in writing. Make a habit of writing short, *dated MFRs* (Memos For Record) of important conversations (such as, "June 2 — buyers' agent said that he'll have loan approval by Friday," "June 12 — buyers asked to extend close of escrow one week," and so on).

_____

_____

_____

• **Make sure deadlines are met.** Real estate contracts are filled with deadlines for everything from contingency removals and deposit increases to the ultimate deadline, your close of escrow. Failure to meet each and every deadline can have dreadful consequences. Your deal may fall apart — you may even end up in a lawsuit. However, most deadlines are remarkably flexible. They can usually be lengthened or shortened by negotiation if the need for revision is properly explained and handled promptly with adequate lead time.

The Negotiating Process

Negotiation is an ongoing process — a series of steps without a neatly defined beginning and end.

Each step in the negotiating process begins by gathering information. After you read this book, you'll understand the various aspects of buying and selling a home. Then you can translate your information into action that generates more information that in turn leads to further action. And so it goes, until you own your dream home or you sell your house.

An offer to purchase

Making an offer to purchase can be stressful for the buyer, and receiving one can be stressful for the seller.

A good real estate agent will draw up a legally solid contract. No standard, universally accepted real estate purchase contract is used throughout the country. On the contrary, purchase contracts vary in length and terms from state to state and, within a state, from one locality to another. When an offer to purchase is made, the buyer's real estate agent should provide a suitable contract for your area.

Although buying and selling a home can be a highly emotional experience, good offers defuse this potentially explosive situation by replacing emotion with facts. Buyers and sellers have feelings that can be hurt. Facts don't. That's why facts are the basis of successful negotiations.

All good offers have three things in common:

- **Good offers are based on the sellers' most important concern: a realistic offering price.** Smart buyers base their offering price on houses (comparable to the seller's house in age, size, condition, and location) that have sold within the past six months. Sellers' asking

prices are often fantasy. Actual sale prices of comparable houses are facts. Focus on facts.

- **Good offers have realistic financing terms.** The
buyer's mortgage's interest rate, loan origination fee,
and time allowed to obtain financing (explained in the
upcoming section on contingencies) must be based on
current lending conditions. Some offers get blown out
of the water because a buyer's loan terms are unrealistic. Focus on facts.

If you, as the buyer, have been prequalified or preap-
proved for a loan, your agent should stress that advantage when you present your offer. This proves to the
sellers that you're a creditworthy buyer who's ready,
willing, and financially able to purchase their house.

- **Good offers don't expect a blank check from the
sellers.** Unless property defects are glaringly obvious,
neither the buyer nor the seller will know whether any
corrective work is needed at the time that the offer is
initially submitted. Under these circumstances, it's
smart to use property-inspection clauses (explained in
the next section) that enable you to reopen negotiations

regarding any necessary corrective work after you've received the inspection reports.

Remember that negotiation is an ongoing process. After the *action* of having an offer accepted, the buyer's property inspectors gather *information.* After they've determined what's actually required in the way of corrective work, the buyer and the seller can renew the negotiations *(action)* armed with hard facts *(information).* This sequence beats wasting time and energy by arguing about the cost to complete corrective work before anyone knows the precise number of dollars needed to do the repairs. *Focus on facts.*

If the sellers agree with the price and terms contained in an offer, they'll sign it. Their agent should give the buyer a signed copy of the offer immediately. At this point, you have what's called a *ratified offer* (that is, a signed or accepted offer). This doesn't mean you own the house or it has been sold. All you can say for now is that a sale is pending.

Contingencies

Most offers to purchase contain extremely important escape clauses known as contingencies, which the buyer builds into the contract to protect herself. A *contingency* is some specific future event that must be satisfied in order for the sale to go through. It gives the buyer the right to pull out of the deal if that event fails to happen. If the buyer doesn't remove a contingency, the sale falls apart, and her deposit money is usually returned.

These two contingencies appear in nearly every offer:

- **Financing:** The buyer can pull out of the deal if the loan specified in your contract isn't approved.

- **Property inspections:** The buyer can pull out of the deal if she doesn't approve the inspection reports or can't reach an agreement with the sellers about how to handle any necessary repairs.

Buyers, don't go overboard with contingencies if you're competing for the property with several other buyers. Sellers, especially in strong real estate markets, don't like offers with lots of contingencies. From their perspective, the more contingencies in an offer, the more likely the deal is to fall apart. Buyers must balance the need to protect themselves with the compelling need to have the offer accepted. Keep contingency time frames realistic but short. Resolve as many simple questions as possible before submitting the offer.

Here's a typical loan contingency:

Conditioned [the magic word] upon buyer getting a 30-year, fixed-rate mortgage secured by the property in the amount of 80 percent of the purchase price. Said loan's interest rate shall not exceed 6.0 percent. Loan fees/points shall not exceed 2 percent of loan amount. If buyer can't obtain such financing within 30 days from acceptance of this offer, buyer must notify seller in writing of buyer's election to cancel this contract and have buyer's deposits returned.

Buyers should include a provision in the contract that specifically states that contingencies must be removed in writing. Doing so should eliminate confusion between the buyer and the seller regarding whether a contingency has been satisfied.

Counteroffers

It's highly unlikely that the sellers will accept an offer as it's originally written. Even if they love the offering price, they'll probably tweak the offer here and there to make it acceptable to them. Sellers use *counteroffers* to fine-tune the price, terms, and conditions of offers they receive.

Negotiating price

Suppose a buyer offers $275,000 for a house she likes, and she asks to close escrow 30 days after the sellers accept the offer. Because the sellers had the house listed at $289,500, they think the offering price is a mite low. Furthermore, they need six weeks to relocate.

Instead of rewriting the entire offer, the sellers give the buyer a counteroffer. It states that they're willing to accept all the terms and conditions of the offer except that they want $285,000 and six weeks after acceptance to close escrow.

The ball's in the buyer's court once again. She doesn't mind a six-week close of escrow, but she doesn't want to pay more than $280,000, so she gives the sellers a *counter-counteroffer* to that effect.

_____

_____

_____

Now only one bone of contention remains: the price. The sellers come back with a *firm* $284,000. The buyer grudgingly responds at $281,000 and instructs her agent to make it clear to the sellers that she won't go any higher. Two can play the *firm* game.

If the buyer really wants the house, this phase of the game can be nerve-racking. The buyer worries about another buyer making the sellers a better offer and stealing the house away while she is trying to get the price down that last $3,000. The sellers are equally concerned that they'll lose the buyer by pushing too hard for the final $3,000. The buyer doesn't want to pay a penny more than she has to. The sellers don't want to leave any money on the table.

The buyer and the sellers are tantalizingly close to agreement on price. The buyer's offering price and the sellers' asking price are both factually based on recent sales of comparable houses in the neighborhood. So why the deadlock? Because sometimes the same facts can lead to different conclusions.

An equitable way to resolve this type of impasse is to split the difference fifty-fifty. If the sellers use this technique, they'll come back with a $282,500 offer — down $1,500 from their *firm* asking price of $284,000 and up $1,500 from the buyer's *firm* offering price of $281,000. The mutual $1,500 concession equals less than 1 percent of the home's fair market value based on a $282,500 sale price. That's pinpoint accuracy in a real estate transaction.

Splitting the difference won't work in all situations. It is, however, a fair way to quickly resolve relatively small differences of opinion (a few percent or less of the home's price) so you can make a deal and get on with your life.

Defining time frames

Good contingencies always have precisely defined time frames within which buyers must complete a specified action or drop out of the contract. A seller should never accept an open-ended contingency. For example, if buyers want their parents to inspect the house but don't specify *when* that inspection will take place, the seller should counter with "parental visit shall take place not more than 3 days after offer is accepted." Be realistic but brisk when setting time frames. As a rule, the faster a seller closes buyer escape hatches, the better. As the seller, you don't want your house off the market any longer than is absolutely necessary.

Sellers should think twice before accepting an offer that's subject to the buyers selling their present house before buying theirs. This is the ultimate open-ended contingency. It stigmatizes the sellers' house by driving away other prospective purchasers who can't put their lives on indefinite hold while they wait to see whether the buyers sell their house.

If you, as the seller, accept a "subject to sale of buyer's property" contingency, counter it with a release clause giving you the right to accept a better offer if one comes along. This provision is called a *72-hour clause* because sellers generally specify that they can cancel a deal 72 hours after notifying the buyers that they've gotten another offer.

Why 72 hours? If the new offer comes in on Friday night, 72 hours gets the buyers through the weekend to the next business day in case they need to consult someone who's only available weekdays during normal business hours.

_____

_____

_____

7

Inspections and Insurance

Given how much houses cost today, it's shortsighted not to have the home you plan to purchase carefully inspected before buying it. Skipping inspections to save a few bucks could be the most expensive mistake you ever make. Think of your biggest financial fiasco ever and multiply it by a hundred. That gives you some idea of the magnitude of the mistake you may make if you buy a home without first having it *thoroughly* inspected from foundation to roof.

Conducting Thorough Inspections

A home's physical condition greatly affects its value. You'd feel horrible if you paid top dollar for a home that you thought was in tiptop shape and discovered after you bought it that the house was riddled with expensive defects. Yet unless you're a professional property inspector, you probably don't have the faintest idea how much corrective work a house needs simply by looking at it.

Most states require that sellers and real estate agents make full, immediate disclosure to prospective buyers of all *known* mechanical, structural, and legal problems associated with owner-occupied residential property.

Don't be lulled into a false sense of complacency. *Latent defects* — hidden problems that sellers and their agents aren't aware of regarding the home you're buying — can get you into a heap of budget-busting trouble after you complete your purchase.

All properties should be inspected

Overinspecting a house is much better than underinspecting it. Suppose you spend $350 to have the home you want to buy completely inspected by a qualified inspector, and you find out that nothing is wrong with it. Did you waste your money? No. You can sleep soundly, knowing that your home doesn't need any corrective work.

If, conversely, you skip the inspection to save $350 and later discover that your house needs $35,000 worth of repairs, you end up spending $100 in repairs for every dollar that you "saved."

Here's a list of properties that *must* be inspected prior to purchase:

- **Used houses:** You're most likely to order inspections if your "new" home is someone else's used house. Obviously, the older the house, the greater the likelihood that you'll find defects in its mechanical and structural systems.

- **New houses:** Even if you're buying a newly constructed, never-been-lived-in home, having it thoroughly inspected is wise. Just because the building is new doesn't guarantee that it was built properly. Brand-new houses often have construction flaws, sometimes major ones.

- **Condominiums:** You need an inspection before buying a condominium. Don't forget that when you buy a condo, you're also buying into the entire building in which your condo is located. As a co-owner of the building, you must pay your proportional share of the cost for corrective work required in common areas, such as the roof, heating system, or foundation.

- **Townhouses, cooperative apartments, and other forms of co-ownership property:** See the preceding bullet point about condominiums. Shared ownership requires a property inspection.

All properties need inspecting. Period. Inspect detached residences, attached residences, single-family dwellings, multifamily dwellings, condos, co-ops, townhouses, and anything else that has a foundation and a roof. If you're spending big bucks for a property, protect your investment by having it inspected.

_____

_____

_____

Two types of defects: Patent and latent

Property defects come in two general categories: patent and latent.

- *Patent defects* are out in the open for the world to see. You don't need a professional property inspector to point out glaringly obvious stuff like water stains on the ceiling, cracks in the wall, or a flooded basement. You do, however, need a trained professional to tell you whether these defects are signs of major problems or merely inconsequential blemishes.

- *Latent defects* are out of sight — behind walls or concealed in inaccessible areas under the house or up in the attic, away from casual observation. These defects can be even more financially devastating than patent defects because they're hidden. Faulty wiring, termite damage, a cracked heat exchanger in the furnace, and health- and safety-code problems (such as lead in the water pipes and asbestos insulation) are some examples of latent physical flaws. You must find latent defects or literally pay the consequences.

_____

_____

_____

Patent defect red flags

You can spot the danger signs of possibly serious structural problems even if you've never had any special inspection training, as long as you know what to look for as you walk through a property. Although we advocate that you hire a professional property inspector, here's a list of red flags that every prospective home buyer should be able to spot:

- **Cracks:** Check the property's foundation, interior walls, exterior retaining walls, fireplace, chimney, concrete floors (basement, garage, back porch, and the like), driveway, and sidewalk for large cracks. Any crack that you can stick a pencil into is a large crack. Watch for vertical cracks on any walls and long horizontal or diagonal cracks on exterior walls.

- **Moisture:** Look for water stains on ceilings, walls, and floors. Feel basement walls for dampness. Sniff out the source of moldy smells. Check for drainage problems inside and out by looking for standing water. A sump pump in the basement or garage is a red flag waving to get your attention.

_____

_____

_____

- **Stickiness:** All doors (exterior, interior, garage, and cabinets) and windows should open and close easily.

- **Looseness:** You shouldn't be able to see daylight around windows, doors, or skylights.

- **Unevenness:** Floors shouldn't slope, and walls shouldn't bulge.

- **Insects:** If the house you're buying is made of wood or wood and stucco, it may have problems with wood-destroying insects or organisms. Mud tubes along a house's foundation or in its basement are a sign of termite infestation. Look carefully at those areas of the property that come into contact with the earth — foundation, decks, garage, and fencing — for signs of decayed or rotted wood.

Before you have the property inspected, discuss any red flags you discover with your property inspector. Let the pro check them out to see whether they're major problems or relatively minor flaws that you can quickly and inexpensively correct. A sticking front door, for example, can indicate either that the house has expensive foundation problems or simply that the door absorbed moisture because it wasn't properly sealed.

Types of property inspections

What inspections should you get to protect your investment? That depends on what area of the country you live in, how the building in question is constructed, and what you plan to do to the property after buying it. Here are the three most common types of inspections — which we recommend be done *after* you have an accepted offer to purchase but *before* removing your inspection contingencies:

- **Prepurchase interior- and exterior-components inspection:** No matter whether you're buying a wood-frame cottage in the country or an urban condo in a 20-story steel-and-concrete building, you need a complete inspection of the property's interior and exterior. The inspection should cover such areas as the roof and gutters, plumbing, electrical work, heating and cooling systems, insulation, smoke detectors, kitchen, bathroom, and foundation. The inspection should also point out health, safety, and environmental hazards. This type of inspection usually takes several hours to complete and costs $300 to $600, depending on how large the property is and the inspection's length and degree of detail.

- **Pest control inspection:** Warm climates, such as in the South and West, are a mixed blessing. You're not the only one who loves warm, balmy weather. So do termites, carpenter ants, powderpost beetles, dry rot, fungi, and other wood-munching infestations or infections. If these are a problem in your area, you also need a pest control inspection. These inspections generally cost $150 to $400.

Pest control inspections are very limited in scope — the inspectors check for property damage caused only by wood-destroying insects (infestations) and organisms (infections, such as dry rot and fungi). If you get a pest control inspection, it should be in addition to your prepurchase interior- and exterior-components inspection — not in lieu of it.

Inspecting inspectors

When you are ready to hire an inspector, hire someone who only does inspections. A growing number of property inspectors are exactly that: professional property inspectors, not contractors.

_____

_____

_____

Professional property inspectors are specifically trained to do inspections and only inspections; they make their living solely from inspection fees. They don't do corrective work, which eliminates the temptation to find unnecessary corrective work during their inspections.

Selecting your inspector

How can you find a qualified home inspector? Ask friends and business associates who've recently bought homes whom they used for their property inspections. Get a list of home inspectors from a real estate agent. If several sources recommend the same inspector, you've likely found a good one.

The American Society of Home Inspectors (ASHI) is a professional association of independent home inspectors. Just because an inspector is an ASHI member doesn't guarantee that you'll get a good inspection, but it certainly increases the likelihood that you'll be working with a qualified professional. All ASHI-certified members have performed at least 250 property inspections and have passed two written proficiency exams as a prerequisite of membership. ASHI members must also adhere to ASHI's standards of practice, continuing education requirements, and code of ethics. To find members in your area, call ASHI at 800-743-2744 or visit its website at www.ashi.org.

We recommend that you interview several property inspectors before hiring one. Here are questions to help you select the best inspector:

- **Are you a full-time, professional property inspector?** Only one answer is acceptable: Yes.

- **What can you tell me about your company?** Discuss the company's size and how long it has been in business.

- **Do you carry errors and omissions insurance?** Errors and omissions insurance covers the possibility that a property inspection could miss some problems. If an inspector makes an error that costs you big bucks, errors and omissions insurance can help make amends.

- **How many inspections do you personally perform each year?** Although the average number of inspections varies from area to area, active inspectors usually conduct between 150 and 400 inspections per year. Find out whether the inspector works primarily in the area in which the property you want to have inspected is located and is thus familiar with local codes, local regulations, and local problems (such as floods, earth-quakes, tornadoes, and the like).

- **Do you hold any special licenses or certifications?**
  Property inspectors usually have a background in some related field, such as construction, engineering, architecture, electricity, plumbing, or insurance claim adjusting. This diversity adds extra insights to their inspections. Membership in ASHI or another trade association for property inspectors indicates at least a minimal knowledge of home inspection procedures.

- **What's the scope of your prepurchase inspection?**
  Make sure that the inspection covers all the property's major structural and mechanical systems, inside and out, from foundation to roof.

- **How long will your inspection take?** Time spent at the site is an important consideration. This inspection isn't a race. It usually takes two or three hours to thoroughly inspect a home of average size.

- **What type of report will I receive?** You must receive a detailed description of your specific property's mechanical and structural condition. You need a narrative report, written in plain English, that clearly explains the implications of its findings.

Get a sample report from each inspector you interview. The best way to see whether a company writes good reports is to read one so you can draw your own conclusion.

- **Do you mind if I tag along during your inspection?** Good inspectors insist that you be present during the property inspection.

- **Will your report include an estimate of the cost to do your recommended corrective work?** This is a trick question. If the inspector says yes, don't use the inspector. Good professional property inspectors do only inspections. They don't do corrective work. Good inspectors help you establish repair costs by referring you to three or four reputable contractors, roofers, electricians, and other repair people that you can contact for corrective-work quotes. Because there's usually more than one way to fix a defect, you have to decide how best to deal with a problem after you've consulted the appropriate repair people.

- **How much does your inspection cost?** This is generally the first question that buyers ask when shopping for a property inspector. This is no time to be penny-wise and pound-foolish. Quality inspections cost more than quickie, one-size-fits-all, checklist inspections because they're worth a lot more. Ultimately, because fees charged by good inspectors are usually pretty much the same, you'll probably end up using the correct criteria to select your inspector: compatibility and competence.

- **Would you mind if I call some of your recent customers for references?** Good property inspectors are happy to give you names and phone numbers of their satisfied customers. Bad inspectors may balk at providing references or direct you to people they know will say something positive about them. Be sure to check at least three references per inspector in the town where the property is located. Ask the references whether, after close of escrow, they discovered any major defects that their inspector missed and whether they'd use their inspector again.

Optimizing your inspection

Here are guidelines for getting the biggest bang out of the bucks that you invest in a prepurchase property inspection:

- **Always make your offer to purchase a house subject to your review and approval of the inspection reports.** Doing so gives you the opportunity to either negotiate a credit or price reduction for corrective work that's discovered during the inspections or, if you want, get out of the deal.

  See whether the sellers have any presale inspection reports that they ordered or any copies of inspection reports generated by previous prospective buyers. If so, give the reports to your inspector to call attention to possible problem areas. Have your agent order a permit search on the property to find out whether electrical, plumbing, or other repairs or improvements have been made.

  Suppose that the sellers give you a presale inspection report that they ordered just before putting their house on the market. It says that their house is in perfect condition. You could save money by relying on their report instead of getting your own. Should you? No. Always pay for your own inspection by an inspector of your own choosing.

- **Read your property inspector's report carefully.** If you don't see some defects listed in the report that your inspector specifically mentioned during the inspection, call the inspector to find out why. By the same token, don't be the least bit shy about calling your inspector to get a detailed explanation of anything you don't completely understand in the report.

- **To minimize the cost of corrective repairs, get bids on the job from several reputable, licensed contractors.** Never try to save money by using unlicensed contractors to do the work without permits. Doing so is usually illegal, can create health and safety problems, and can adversely affect your home's resale value.

- **Use your property inspector during the contractor bidding process.** If the contractors have questions regarding items discussed in the inspection report, refer them to the report's author for clarification.

If your agent or the seller offers to pay for a *home warranty plan* or *home protection plan* (that is, a service contract that covers some of your home's major systems and appliances), it wouldn't be gracious of you to turn down a freebie. Never accept such a plan in lieu of an inspection, however.

Don't expect your inspections to eliminate all future maintenance problems. Anything in your home that can break or leak will break or leak, sooner or later. Repairs come with homeownership. After closing on your home purchase, normal upkeep is your responsibility.

Insuring Your Home

Nobody likes to spend money for insurance. But if something could cause you a financial catastrophe, you should insure against that risk. The point of insurance is that you spend a relatively small amount of money to protect against losing a great deal of money. For example, if your home burns to the ground and it's not insured, you could be out tens (if not hundreds) of thousands of dollars.

Here are the types of insurance that you need to have in place *before* you purchase your dream home.

Homeowners insurance

When you buy a home, most lenders require that you purchase homeowners insurance. Even if you're one of those rare people who can buy a home with cash without borrowing money, you should carry homeowners coverage. Why?

- First, your home and the personal property (furniture, carpets, clothing and jewelry, computers, dishes, and the like) in your home would cost a small fortune to replace out of your own pocket.

- Second, your home can lead to a lawsuit. If someone were injured or killed in your home, you could be sued for tens or hundreds of thousands of dollars.

The following sections tell how to get the homeowners coverage you need.

The cost of rebuilding

If your home is destroyed, which most frequently happens from fires, your insurance policy should pay for the cost of rebuilding your home. The portion of your policy that takes care of this loss is the *dwelling coverage* section. The amount of this coverage should be equal to the cost of rebuilding the home you own. The cost to rebuild should be based on the square footage of your home. Your policy's dwelling coverage amount shouldn't be based on what you paid for the home or the amount of your mortgage.

Get a policy that includes a *guaranteed replacement cost provision*. This provision ensures that the insurance company will rebuild the home, even if the cost of construction is more than the policy coverage. If the insurance company underestimates your dwelling coverage, the company has to eat the difference.

Ask the insurers you're speaking with how they define *guaranteed replacement cost coverage* — each insurer defines it differently. The most generous policies, for example, pay for the home's full replacement cost, no matter how much the replacement ends up costing. Other insurers set limits — for example, they agree to pay up to 120 percent of your policy's total dwelling coverage.

Lawsuit protection

Liability insurance protects you against lawsuits arising from bad things that happen to others while they're on your property.

Carry enough liability insurance to protect at least two times the value of your assets. Although the chances of being sued are remote, remember that if you're sued, the financial consequences can be staggering.

Personal property protection

On a typical homeowners policy, the amount of personal property coverage is usually set at about 50 to 75 percent of the amount of dwelling coverage. If you're a condo owner, however, you generally need to choose a specific dollar amount for the personal property coverage you want.

Some policies come with *personal property replacement guarantees* that pay you for the replacement cost of an item rather than for the actual value of a used item at the time that it's damaged or stolen. If this feature isn't part of the standard policy sold by your insurer, you may want to purchase it as a *rider* (add-on provision), if such a rider is available.

_____

_____

_____

If you ever need to file a claim, having documentation of your personal property helps. No matter how you document your belongings, be sure to place this documentation somewhere outside your home. A list or video isn't going to do you much good if it's in your home and your house goes up in a smoke during a fire or is irreparably damaged in a flood.

Title insurance

In theory, you can go down to the local county recorder's office and find out who owns any piece of property in the county simply by checking the public record. In fact, all sorts of irregularities in the history of the various people who've owned the property since it was originally constructed can affect a property's title — irregularities that are difficult or impossible to find, no matter how diligently you comb the public records.

Here are some causes of these hidden risks to titles:

• **Secret spouses:** A seller may claim to be single when, in fact, he or she is secretly married in another state. Or perhaps the seller was divorced in a community property state where, through marriage, one spouse obtains a legal interest in property held individually by the other spouse. Whatever the reason, sometimes a present or former spouse no one knew about will show up out of the blue and file a claim against the property. This explains why title company representatives are so curious about your marital status. They must know whether you're single, married, divorced, or widowed to keep ownership records accurate.

- **Undisclosed heirs:** When property owners die without wills, probate courts must decide who their rightful heirs are. Court decisions may not be binding on heirs who aren't notified of the proceeding. Undiscovered heirs sometimes magically appear and claim that they now own the property in question.

- **Questionable competency:** Minors and people adjudged to be mentally incompetent can't enter into binding contracts unless their court-appointed guardians or conservators handle the transaction. If, for example, the seller was a minor or was mentally incompetent when a deed was signed, the transaction may be voidable or invalid.

- **Goofs:** This is a highly technical, catchall category for human errors. It covers everything from clerks who overlook liens recorded against property (liens for unpaid federal and state income taxes or local property taxes, for example) and other important documents while doing title searches, to surveyors who incorrectly establish property boundaries. Honest mistakes create many title problems.

- **Forgery and fraud:** Sellers are sometimes fraudulently impersonated. By the same token, signatures can be forged on documents. Escrow officers demand identification to establish that you are who you claim to be.

- **Name confusion:** A lot of title problems result from people having names similar (or identical) to the buyer's name or seller's name. Even though you prove that you are who you claim you are, you also have to prove who you aren't. If you have a fairly common last name, you'll probably have to fill out a Statement of Information to help the title company distinguish you from other people with names like yours.

What title insurance does

Many people who buy homes spend hundreds of dollars for title insurance without understanding what they're getting for their money. *Title insurance* assures homeowners and mortgage lenders that a property has a marketable *(valid)* title. If someone makes a claim that threatens your ownership of the home, the title insurance company protects you and the lender against loss or damage, according to the terms and provisions of your respective title insurance policies.

Most of your title insurance premium pays for research to determine who legally owns the property that you want to buy and to find out whether any unpaid tax liens or judgments are recorded against it. Because title companies do a good job of eliminating title risks *before* folks buy property, only about 10 percent of the premium goes toward indemnifying homeowners against title claims *after* the close of escrow.

The title insurance premium that you pay at close of escrow is the one and only title insurance premium that you'll have to pay, *unless you refinance your mortgage.*

Title insurance deals with your risk of loss from *past* problems (such as unpaid property tax liens or forgery in the chain of title) that *may* exist at the time that your policy is issued. Because your policy covers the past, which is a fixed event, you pay only one title insurance premium *as long as you keep your original mortgage.*

Two kinds of title insurance

As a homeowner, you have a choice of two kinds of *owners* title insurance. Depending on the extent of the coverage that you desire, you can either get a standard coverage policy or an extended coverage policy.

- *A standard title insurance policy* is less expensive than an extended policy because its coverage is more limited. Standard policies are limited to certain off-record risks (such as fraud in the chain of title, defective recordings, and competency), plus *recorded* (at the local county recorder's office) tax assessments, judgments, and other property defects that a search of public records can uncover.

- *Extended title insurance policies* cover everything that standard policies do, plus they provide expanded coverage for off-record risks that could be discovered through a property inspection or by making inquiries of people in actual possession of the property, as well as defects such as *unrecorded* (never recorded at the county recorder's office) leases or contracts of sale.

Title insurance costs vary greatly, depending on the geographic area in which your home is located, the home's purchase price, and the type of coverage you get. In addition to the owners policy that we recommend you purchase to protect your investment, most lenders will insist that you buy a policy to protect the mortgage lender against loss on the loan amount.

Local custom and practice determine who usually pays for title insurance. In some parts of the country, custom dictates that the buyer pays for it. In other areas, however, the seller pays the title insurance premium, or buyers and sellers split the cost fifty-fifty.

8

Escrow

After vetting dozens of houses (if you're a buyer) and potential buyers (if you're a seller), haggling over price, and agreeing to sales terms, the big day draws near. But don't breathe a sigh of relief just yet. You still have work to do, and there's still time for things to go wrong.

However, the information in this chapter helps you navigate the last days of the transaction, regardless of whether you are a buyer or a seller. If you follow the advice we offer, the closing process should go smoothly.

The Benefits of Escrow

As soon as possible after the buyer and the seller have a *ratified offer* (that is, a signed contract), all funds, documents, and instructions pertaining to your transaction should be delivered to a neutral third party: the *escrow holder* designated in your purchase agreement. The act of giving these funds, documents, and instructions to the escrow holder constitutes the *escrow*. Depending on the local custom in your area, a lawyer, an escrow firm, or a title company may handle the escrow. Buyers and sellers generally select an escrow holder based on recommendations from their agents. However, as with other companies you choose to do business with in your home buying transaction, escrow fees and service quality vary.

Real estate deals are often characterized by mutual distrust. Whether you're the buyer or the seller, you and the other party need someone whom both of you can trust to hold the stakes while you work through all the resolved and unresolved details in your contract. The escrow holder (also known as the *escrow officer*) is your referee — a neutral third party who shouldn't show any favoritism to either the buyer or the seller.

The Escrow Officer

Your escrow officer is responsible for preparing and reviewing papers related to the transfer of *title* — a legal document that stipulates ownership of the property. This includes getting the papers properly signed, delivered, and made a matter of public record; complying with your lender's funding instructions; ordering a title search; and accounting to the buyer and the seller for their respective money. The escrow officer handles the nitty-gritty paperwork and money details.

When the escrow is opened, the contract will probably be filled with loopholes known as *contingencies* or *conditions of sale*. For example, the contract should be written so the buyer can get out of the deal if he doesn't approve the property inspection reports, or if the seller can't give clear title to the property, or if the buyer can't get a loan.

The escrow officer's job is to receive and follow your instructions.

- As the buyer, don't instruct the escrow officer to give your money to the seller until you're *fully* satisfied that the seller has performed under the contract.

- When you're the seller, be sure to instruct your escrow officer not to give the buyer the title to your property until you're completely satisfied that all terms and conditions of the contract are fulfilled.

Here are some other highlights from your escrow officer's to-do list:

- **Request payoff information:** If the seller has a mortgage, home equity loan, or other liens on the property, the escrow officer contacts the lenders to get the current loan balances and instructions for paying off the various loans at close of escrow.

- **Prepare and record documents:** The escrow officer draws up a grant deed that the seller signs to formally transfer legal title to the buyer. The deed is recorded when escrow closes.

- **Hold and disburse funds:** At close of escrow, the escrow officer uses funds the buyers and their lender put into escrow to make payments required to close the escrow, such as paying off the seller's loans.

- **Prepare estimated and final closing statements:** These documents provide an accounting of all the money that comes into and goes out of escrow.

Ideally, your escrow will go smoothly from start to close. If, however, the escrow officer gets conflicting instructions from the buyer and the seller or lender, the escrow will stop dead in its tracks until the argument is resolved. What kind of conflicting instructions? Disputes about whether the purchase price includes an item of personal property (that is, a refrigerator, a mirror, a light fixture, and the like) are always popular. So are disagreements about whether corrective work should be done before or after close of escrow.

Good escrow officers are worth their weight in gold in times of crisis when the shouting, tears, and threats of lawsuit begin. At moments like this, often only the escrow officer's incredible patience and crisis-mediation skills keep deals glued together.

Paperwork

To avoid truly horrible surprises, pay particular attention to the following reports and statements.

Buyers: Closing costs

We have a detailed itemization of closing costs in Chapter 2. We suggest that you turn to that chapter now and review the information about closing costs, or the following tips won't make much sense.

As soon as possible, get a rough idea of how much money you have to come up with at the close of escrow. Immediately after opening escrow, ask your lender or mortgage broker for a TILA RESPA Integrated Disclosure (TRID) Loan Estimate of your estimated closing costs. Even though it may take several weeks to get actual costs for inspection fees, repair-work credits, homeowners insurance premiums, and the like, at least you'll have a preliminary number that you can fine-tune as additional information becomes available. Having the knowledge available in this preliminary statement beats getting hammered by unexpected closing costs a couple of days before the close of escrow.

Estimate the closing expenses on the high side. Overestimating expenses and finding, when actual costs come in, that you don't need as much money to close as you first expected is ideal. The sooner you put a box around your closing costs, the better. Don't react to the situation — control it.

If, like most folks, you must put additional money in escrow just before the close of the transaction, use a cashier's check or a money order, or have your funds wired directly to the escrow to prevent delays. Be sure you stay on top of your bank to ensure that the wire is expedited because banks sometimes drop the ball. Personal checks take time to clear, and credit cards don't cut it in escrows. If you have questions regarding what constitutes *good funds,* ask your escrow officer well in advance of the close of escrow.

Sellers: Estimated closing statement

During your initial contact with the escrow officer, request an estimated closing statement based strictly on your known closing costs at that time and assuming the escrow closes as scheduled. This statement won't be precise. Factors such as whether you'll have to give the buyers a credit for repairs, and if so, how much, have yet to be determined. No matter. At least you have an approximation of your expenses of sale, and that helps you develop a rough idea about the amount of money you may have to spend on your next home.

_____

_____

_____

Get the estimated closing statement updated a week before scheduled close of escrow. At that point, very few questions should remain. You're basically waiting for the clock to tick out. Check your second estimated closing statement extremely carefully, line by line from top to bottom, to be absolutely certain that it accurately reflects your credits and debits.

Buyers and sellers: Preliminary report

Shortly after escrow is opened, you should receive an extremely important document: the *preliminary report* (or *prelim*) from your title company. This report shows who currently owns the property that you want to buy, as well as any money claims (such as mortgage liens, income tax judgments, and property tax assessments) that affect the property. Last but not least, the preliminary title report shows any third-party restrictions and interests — such as condominium covenants, conditions, and restrictions (CC&Rs) — and utility company or private easements that limit your use of the property or some other claim about which you had no information.

The contract should be contingent upon your review and approval of the preliminary report. Look it over carefully. Ask your agent, escrow officer, title company representative, or lawyer to explain anything in the report that you don't understand. Don't be shy — there's no such thing as a dumb question. When you're the buyer, you want to make sure your seller owns the property and there is enough money in the escrow to pay off all the debts that have nothing to do with you.

As per the purchase contract, the buyer should have the right to *reasonably* disapprove of certain claims or restrictions that he doesn't want on the property and to ask the owner to clear them prior to the close of escrow. For example, asking the seller to pay off all debts secured by liens and judgments against the property is reasonable.

Buyers and sellers: Closing Disclosure

When buying a house, you may believe that the most important piece of paper you get when escrow closes is the deed to your new home. When selling your house, you may think that the most valuable piece of paper you get when escrow closes is your check for the proceeds of sale.

From an accounting standpoint, however, the most important piece of paper is the TRID Closing Disclosure that you get from the escrow officer on the day that your escrow actually closes.

If you think of the escrow as a checking account, the final settlement statement is like the account statement. It records all the money that went through the escrow as either a credit or a debit:

- **Credits:** Any money that the buyer put into escrow (such as the initial deposit and down payment) appears as a credit to the account. The buyer may also receive credits from the seller for such things as corrective work repairs and property taxes. And, of course, the buyer's loan is a credit.

    The seller won't have many credits; the biggie is always the credit for the amount of the sale price. The seller may get a credit from the buyers for the unused portion of property taxes that the seller prepaid.

- **Debits:** Funds paid out of escrow are shown as debits. Debits include modest and not-so-modest expenses, such as what the buyer pays the seller for the home, loan fees, homeowners insurance premiums, property inspection fees, the seller's mortgage payoff, real estate commissions, and corrective work credits that the seller grants the buyer.

_____

_____

_____

The buyer meets with the escrow officer several days before close of escrow to sign the loan documents and other papers related to the home purchase. At that time, the buyer receives a more precise TRID Closing Disclosure detailing what the closing costs are if the escrow closes as scheduled. Check this TRID Closing Disclosure *extremely* carefully, line by line and from top to bottom, to be absolutely certain that it accurately reflects the credits and debits.

Escrow officers are human — they sometimes make mistakes. So do other participants in the transaction who may have given the escrow officer incorrect information. When mistakes turn up, they're generally not in the buyer's favor. Pay attention to detail. Review the closing statement and question whatever isn't clear or correct. You need not determine at the time you sign the loan documents precisely what's wrong with the closing statement. Take it home with you, continue inspecting it, and ask the various parties to the transaction to clarify anything you don't understand about it.

The TRID Closing Disclosure is extremely important. Keep a copy for your files — it will come in handy when the time comes to complete your annual income tax return. Some expenses of purchase (such as loan origination fees and property tax payments) are tax deductible. Tax-deductible expenses for the seller include the real estate commission, mortgage prepayment penalties, and property tax payments. Furthermore, the TRID Closing Disclosure establishes the buyer's initial tax (cost) basis in the property. When you sell your property, you may owe capital gains tax on any profit you make by selling the property for more than your cost basis.

December Escrows

As a rule, December is a slow month for home sales. A week or two before Thanksgiving, most buyers switch their attention from houses to holidays and family gatherings, and those buyers typically don't get back onto the home buying track until around Super Bowl Sunday in mid-winter.

 Here are two reasons that you, as a buyer, may decide to buck the trend:

_____

_____

_____

- **Bargain hunting:** When the other buyers drop out of the market, you're the only interested party for sellers who must move soon, or for stubborn sellers who waited too long to get realistic about their asking price. If they must sell, sellers instruct their agents to put the word out that they're willing to deal. If you're a low-baller looking for a deal, now's the time to make your move.

- **Tax deductions:** What you get doesn't matter — what does matter is what you get to keep. Buying a home in December gives you tax deductions that you can use to reduce your federal and state income taxes in that calendar year. Owning a home gives you physical shelter and tax shelter. On your income taxes, you can, for example, write off your loan origination fee (points), mortgage interest, and property taxes that you pay on or before December 31.

Escrows are perverse creatures under even the best of circumstances. They're proof positive of Murphy's Law, which states that whatever can go wrong will — and *always* at the worst possible time. Experienced escrow officers know that nasty surprises can rear their ugly heads whenever you least expect them.

The list of potential surprises is unpleasantly long: missed deadlines, title glitches, problems paying off existing loans, changes in your loan's terms, insufficient funds to close escrow, funds not wired as promised, and so on.

December escrows are particularly perverse. Partying zaps your strength and reduces your effectiveness. People forget to sign papers before leaving on vacation. December 31 is an immutable deadline if you want to close this year for tax purposes. If you end up with a late December escrow, here are some things you (and your real estate agent) should do to make sure you meet your deadline:

- **Stay in touch with your lender.** Lenders need copious documentation to substantiate loan applications. Be sure your lender has all the required documents as soon as possible. Lenders say that lack of follow-up on loan-document verification is a top cause of escrow delays.

- **Don't leave any blank spaces on your loan application.** Draw a line through any section that doesn't apply to you. If you leave a section blank, the lender may assume that you forgot to complete it. And keep a copy of everything you submit in case the originals get lost or you need to refer to the documents when the lender questions something you wrote.

- **Stay in touch with your escrow officer.** Don't let your file get buried in a pile of pending escrows stuck on the corner of your escrow officer's desk. You or your agent should check with the escrow officer periodically to make sure things are going smoothly.

- **Buyers, be available to sign your loan documents.** You may have only 24 to 48 hours after your loan package arrives at the escrow office to sign the documents and return them to the lender. A delay could cost you the loan.

- **Sellers, order loan demands as soon as possible.** You must pay off any of your existing loans that are secured by the property before the buyer can have a new mortgage put on the property. Instruct your escrow officer to order payoff statements on all your existing loans immediately. Lack of receipt of loan payoff statements is a top reason for escrow delays.

- **If you're leaving town for the holidays, tell your agent, lender, and escrow officer well in advance of your departure.** You can usually make special arrangements to close your escrow — no matter where you are — as long as people have advance warning and know how to reach you. The key to success is keeping everyone posted.

- **Check the calendar.** Many offices are open only till noon on Christmas Eve and New Year's Eve. When Christmas Day and New Year's Day fall on Saturday or Sunday, office hours can really get crazy. Be sure to check the holiday office schedule of your agent, lender, escrow officer, and so on. Don't let a holiday office closing derail your deal.

- **Allow time between when you'd like to close and when you must close.** Give yourself maneuvering room to resolve last-minute problems that inevitably appear when you least expect them. Don't schedule your closing on the last business day of the year — you'll have no margin for error if you need to close by year's end.

Follow Through

It's as unfortunate as it is true: Not all open escrows end in home purchases.

Many escrows could have been saved by applying a fundamental principle of life: follow through. Buyers, sellers, and agents often say that a house has been *sold* when the purchase contract is signed. *Not true!* Nothing was sold. The buyer and seller merely ratified an offer.

If you want to buy and move into the home or sell and move out of your home — that is, close escrow — everyone involved in your transaction must follow through on all the details.

9

Deciding to Sell

Selling your house and moving can be an enjoyable (and profitable) experience. Unfortunately, for most people, it isn't. Selling a house not only introduces financial turmoil into most people's lives but also causes them stress.

We're certainly not going to tell you how and where to spend your money — that's your choice. However, we definitely want you to make the most of your money. Unless you're one of the few who has far more money than you can ever possibly spend, we suggest that you prioritize the demands on your money to accomplish your most important financial goals.

Before you decide to move and incur all of the accompanying expenses, think about the impact of that kind of spending on other aspects of your life. The more you spend on housing, the less you'll have for your other goals, such as saving for retirement or taking annual vacations, and the more time you may be forced to spend working.

Do You Really Need to Sell?

Although spending your entire life in the first home you buy is an unlikely prospect, some people do end up living in the same home for 10, 20, even 30 or more years.

If, like most prospective house sellers, you have a choice between staying put and selling, *not* selling has clear advantages. Selling your house and then buying another one takes a great deal of legwork and research on your part. Whether you sell your house yourself or hire an agent, you're going to be heavily involved in getting your house ready for sale and keeping it pristine while it's on the market.

In addition to time, selling your house and buying another one can cost serious money. Between real estate commissions, loan fees, title insurance, transfer tax, and myriad other costs of selling your house and then buying another one, you can easily spend 15 percent or more of the value of the property that you're selling.

Fifteen percent sounds like a lot, doesn't it? Well, consider this: Unless you own your house free and clear of any mortgage debt, your transaction costs are going to consume an even larger percentage of the money you've invested in your home.

Consider this scenario: You're thinking about selling your $240,000 house. If selling your house and buying another one costs you about 15 percent of the first house's value, then you're taking $36,000 out of your sale proceeds. However, if you happen to owe $180,000 on your mortgage, your *equity* in the home — the difference between the amount the house is worth ($240,000) and the amount you owe ($180,000) — is $60,000. Therefore, the $36,000 in transaction costs devours a huge 60 percent of your equity.

Before spending that much of your hard-earned money, make sure you give careful thought and consideration to why you want to sell, the financial consequences of selling, and the alternatives to selling.

Good reasons to stay

Whereas some people have clear and compelling reasons for selling their homes, others do so for the wrong reasons. You don't want to make the financially painful mistake of selling if you don't have to or can't afford to.

_____

_____

_____

The following sections offer reasons why you may be better off staying right where you are.

You're having trouble living within your means

If you're having difficulty making ends meet, and you use high-interest consumer credit, such as credit cards or auto loans, to maintain your desired standard of living, you shouldn't spend more money on housing. Even if you're planning to trade your current house for one of comparable value, you may not be able to afford all the transaction costs of selling and buying.

Even if you don't have consumer debt and you're saving a comfortable portion (10 percent or more) of your current earnings, *don't* assume that you can afford to trade up to a more expensive home. In addition to a higher mortgage payment, you may also face increased property taxes, insurance rates, and home maintenance costs.

A mortgage lender may be willing to finance a loan that enables you to trade up to a more expensive home, but qualifying for a loan doesn't mean that you can *afford* that home (see Chapter 2 for details).

The problems are more in your perceptions

Everybody, at some point, leaps to conclusions based on faulty assumptions or incomplete research in virtually all aspects of their lives. It's no different when deciding to move from one community to another.

Crime and safety are a common area where people have misconceptions. Some communities often make the evening news with graphic stories and film footage of crimes. Statistically, however, most crimes committed in a given city or town occur in fairly small geographic areas. Local police departments tabulate neighborhood crime rates. If you're concerned about crime and safety, don't guess; get the facts by contacting your local police department and asking them how to obtain the data.

Schools are another hot-button issue. In some areas, people make blanket statements condemning all public schools. They also insist that if you live in such-and-such town or city, you must send your children to private school if you want them to get a good education. The reality is that you can find good and bad public schools and good and bad private schools.

Selling won't solve the problem(s)

Avoiding problems is another human tendency. Some home-owners decide that instead of correcting costly problems with their home, they'll sell it to an unsuspecting buyer instead.

However, when you attempt to sell your home without disclosing known defects — a major legal no-no — you will be found out by smart buyers who learn about the problems from inspectors they hire to check out the property.

Instead of selling to avoid dealing with the problems, make the repairs (see the following section).

You can fix some or all of the problems

You can address quite a number of shortcomings in your home less expensively than buying a new home.

If you think home improvement projects are going to be too expensive, do some rough calculations to determine the cost of selling your current house and then buying another. Remember, you can easily spend 15 percent of the house's value on all the transaction costs of selling and then buying again.

Instead of trading houses, spend those transaction dollars on improving the home you currently own. Just be careful not to turn your home into a castle if all the surrounding houses are shacks. Overimproving your property can be an expensive mistake. You don't want to make such dramatic improvements to your house that you'll own the most expensive house on the block. You'll have difficulty recouping the cost of the improvements in the form of a higher house sale price.

Some problems and defects are more easily fixed and more worth fixing than others. When you're deciding whether to fix problems or move away from them, consider these important issues:

- **What's the payback?** Some home remodeling projects may pay for or come close to paying for themselves because they increase your home's value by enough to make up for most or even all the cost of the improvement(s).

  Generally speaking, projects that increase the cosmetic appeal or usability of living space tend to be more financially worthwhile than projects that don't. For example, consider painting and recarpeting a home versus fixing its foundation. The former projects are visible and, if done well, enhance a home's value; the latter project doesn't add to the visible appeal of the home or usability of living space. If, however, you *must* do foundation repairs or the house will collapse, spend your money on the foundation.

- **How intrusive will the work be?** As you know, money isn't everything. In addition to costing more than most parties expect, contracting work almost always takes longer than everyone expects. Ask yourself and others who've endured similar projects: How much will this project disrupt my life? Your contract with the contractor should include financial penalties for not finishing on time.

Reasons to consider selling

If you're in a situation where you really *need* to sell, as opposed to wanting to sell, by all means put your house on the market. And if you *want* to sell, and can *afford* to do so, you should go for it as well. The following sections offer some solid reasons for selling.

You can afford to trade homes

Your desire to sell your current house and buy another one may be driven by a force as frivolous as sheer boredom.

_____

_____

_____

But if you can afford to sell and buy again, and you know what you're getting into, why not?

Now, defining *afford* is important. By *afford,* we mean that you've identified your personal and financial goals and you've calculated that the cost of trading houses won't compromise those goals (like saving for retirement or your children's college education).

You need to move for your job

Some people find that at particular points in their lives they need to move to take advantage of a career opportunity. For example, if you want to be involved with technology companies, certain regions of the country offer far greater opportunities than others.

When you lack employment, paying bills is difficult, especially the costs involved in home ownership. If you've lost your job or your employer demands that you relocate to keep your job, you may feel a real need to move, especially in a sluggish economy.

Moving for a better job (or simply for *a* job) is a fine thing to do. However, some people fool themselves into believing that a higher-paying job or a move to an area with lower housing costs will put them on an easier financial street. You must consider all the costs of living in a new area versus your current area before deciding that moving to a new community is financially wise.

Also consider that you may be overlooking career opportunities in your area. Just because your employer offers you a better job to get you to relocate doesn't mean you can't bargain for a promotion and stay put geographically.

You're having (or will have) financial trouble

Sometimes people fall on difficult financial times because of an unexpected event. You may develop serious health problems that require you to move into a house that is more accessible for your condition. Or your marriage may fall apart, and you can't afford to stay in the home on only your income.

In addition to unexpected events, some people simply live beyond their means and can't keep their heads above the financial water of large mortgage payments and associated housing costs. Sometimes people get bogged down with additional consumer debt because they stretched themselves too much when buying their home.

Selling your house and moving to a lower-cost housing option may be necessary. On the other hand, if you can bring your spending under control and pay off those consumer debts, maybe you can afford to remain in your present home. Be sure you're being honest with yourself and realistic about your ability to accomplish your goals given your continuing housing expenses.

You're retiring

If you decide to retire, you may find yourself with more house than you need, or you may want to move to a less costly area. Instead of trading up, you may consider trading down.

You can free up some of the cash you've tied up in your current house and use that money to help finance your retirement by moving to a less expensive home. If you're otherwise happy with where you're currently living, don't think you must trade down to a less expensive home simply to tap the equity in your current property. You can tap your home's equity through other methods, such as taking out a reverse mortgage.

Housing Market Health

Your personal financial situation is an important factor in deciding whether and when to sell your house, but the state of your local housing market may also influence your decision. Read the following sections to understand how the housing market can affect your sale.

Selling in a depressed housing market

No one likes to lose money. If you scraped and saved for years for the down payment to buy a home, finding out that your house is worth less than the amount you paid for it can be quite a blow. Between the decline in the market value of your home and the selling costs, you may possibly even lose your entire invested down payment.

Some homeowners find themselves *upside down*, which means that the mortgage on the house exceeds the amount for which the house can be sold. In other words, upside-down homeowners have to pay money to sell their houses because they've lost more than their original down payment.

When deciding whether to sell in a depressed market, consider the factors discussed in the following sections.

If you still have adequate equity

Although your local real estate market may have recently declined, if you've owned your house long enough or made a large enough down payment, you still may be able to net a good deal of cash by selling. If you can make enough money to enable yourself to buy another home, don't worry that your local real estate market may currently be depressed. As long as the sale fits in with your overall financial situation, sell your house and get on with your life.

All real estate markets go through up cycles and down cycles. Over the long term, however, housing prices tend to increase. So if you sell a house or two during a down market, odds are you'll also sell a house or two during better market conditions. And if you're staying in the same area or moving to another depressed housing market, you're simply trading one reduced-price house for another. If you're moving to a more expensive market or a market currently doing better than the one you're leaving, be sure that spending more on housing doesn't compromise your long-term personal and financial goals.

If you lack enough money to buy your next home

Sometimes homeowners find themselves in a situation where, if they sell, they won't have enough money to buy their next home. If you find yourself in such a circumstance, first clarify whether you *want* or *need* to sell:

- If you *want* to sell but don't *need* to and can avoid selling for a while, wait it out. Otherwise, if you sell and then don't have adequate money to buy your next home, you may find yourself in the unfortunate position of being a renter when the local real estate market turns the corner and starts improving again. So you'll have sold low and later be forced to buy high. You'll need to have an even greater down payment to get back into the market, or you'll be forced to buy a more modest house.

- If you *need* to sell, you have a tougher road ahead of you. You must hope that the real estate market where you buy won't rocket ahead while you're trying to accumulate a larger down payment. However, you may also want to look into methods for buying a home with a smaller down payment. For example, a benevolent family member may help you out, or you may decide to take out one of the low-down-payment loans that some mortgage lenders offer. If prices do rise at a fast rate, you can either set your sights on a different market or lower your expectations for the kind of home you're going to buy.

Selling during a strong market

What could be better than selling your house during a time of rising or already-elevated home prices? If you can afford the transaction costs of selling your current house and buying another home, and if the costs of the new home fit within your budget and financial goals, go for it.

Just be careful of two things:

- Don't get greedy and grossly overprice your house. You may end up getting less from the sale than you expected, and the sale is likely to take much longer than if you'd priced the property fairly. If you price your house too high, when you finally drop the price to the right range, you may face lower offers because your house has the stigma of being old on the market. In Chapter 12, we detail how to price your house for a quick sale that gets you top dollar.

- If you're staying in your current strong market or moving to another strong market, be careful about timing the sale of your current house and the purchase of your next one. For example, you probably don't want to sell and then spend months bidding unsuccessfully on other homes. You may get stuck renting for a while and need to make an additional move; such costs can eat up the cash from your recent sale and interfere with your ability to afford your next home. In Chapter 11, we explain how to time the sale of your house and the subsequent purchase of your new home.

10

The Economics of Selling

You may need to get a certain amount of money from the sale of your house, or at least know before you can close on a deal how much you'll receive. Although it's an inexact science, there's no reason you can't reasonably *estimate* your expected proceeds of sale.

Take the time to understand the particular probable proceeds of sale under the following scenarios:

- **You're strapped for cash because you want to buy a more expensive home.** You need to know *before* you sell if you'll have enough money to complete your next purchase. If you don't know this amount, the worst-case scenario is that the sale of your current house doesn't leave you enough money to buy your next one. Although you probably won't end up homeless, you may end up renting for a while and having to make an extra move, or having to scrounge around at the last minute for more money.

- **You're trading down because you need more money for retirement.** Perhaps you want to receive a certain amount of money from your house sale to afford a particular retirement standard of living. If you're not realistic about how much cash you'll net from the sale, you may end up wasting a great deal of time and money on a sale that yields less cash than you need or expect.

- **You're relocating, in part, because of finances.** If you have a choice about taking a job in another part of the country, you may be tempted to relocate if you think that you'll be more comfortable financially. However, if you're assuming or guessing that you'll be better off in the new area, you may be wrong. You need to gather and review the facts before you move.

Estimated Sale Price

The price at which you can sell your house is the biggest factor in determining how much money you'll be able to put into your pocket from selling your house. The estimated sale price, unfortunately, is also the hardest number to pin down.

You shouldn't allow your *needs* to dictate the price at which you list your house for sale (see Chapter 12). Prospective buyers don't care about your needs, wants, or desires. Your house's asking price should be based on the house's worth, which sometimes may not be to your liking. Your house's worth is best determined by examining the recent sale prices of comparable houses. A good real estate agent can put together a comparable market analysis for you.

Estimated house sale price	$ _____
– Closing costs	– $ _____
– Mortgage payoff	– $ _____
– Moving costs	– $ _____
= Estimated proceeds from house sale	= $ _____

Closing Costs

Selling a house costs a good deal of money. Generally, expect to pay about 7 to 10 percent of the house's sale price in various closing costs for which you, as the seller, may be responsible.

A *closing cost* is an expense that you incur in the sale of your house and that reduces the total money you receive from the sale. The typical closing costs include

- **Real estate agent commissions:** If you're selling your house through real estate agents, they typically take a commission of 5 to 6 percent of the selling price. The commission percentage you pay is negotiable and may be somewhat lower on higher-priced properties.

- **Repairs:** Unless you've taken really good care of your house over the years, or you're selling in a strong local real estate market, you can also expect to pay for some corrective work. For example, in some communities, you may need a pest control and dry rot clearance to sell your property. Inspections of your property may uncover building code violations, such as faulty electrical wiring or plumbing problems, that you must repair. You need to consider having your house inspected before listing it for sale (see Chapter 7 for more info).

- **Transfer tax:** Some cities and towns whack you with a transfer tax when you sell your house. Such taxes typically are based on the property's sale price. Check with your real estate agent or your local tax collector's office to get an idea about your community's transfer tax rates.

- **Prorated property taxes:** Depending on the date you close on the sale of your house, you may owe money to bring your property tax payments up-to-date. In most towns and cities, unless you're delinquent with your payments, you probably won't owe more than six months of property taxes. In fact, because many communities require that you pay your property taxes in advance of the period that the payments cover, you may find that you're owed a refund of taxes from your property's buyer.

  Because you can't predict the date your house will sell, estimating the amount that you may owe in property taxes at closing is difficult. You do know, however, whether you have to pay your taxes well in advance. If your local community has such a pay-in-advance payment system or you wait until the last minute to pay your taxes or make delinquent payments, you may want to budget three months or so of property taxes as a closing cost.

- **Possible credits:** If you've paid ahead on your property taxes, you may get a "refund" from the buyer of your house. You may also get a refund from your homeowners insurance company for the unused portion of your homeowners policy. And, finally, if you put less than 20 percent down when you originally purchased the house, your lender may have required that you pay a portion of your property taxes and homeowners insurance in advance each month and then held these payments in an impound account. (An *impound account* refers to money held in a trust account, established by the lender, that is used to pay property taxes and insurance premiums on your behalf when they're due.) The lender refunds the unused funds from your impound account money when the sale is complete.

Do the necessary research for the above expenses if you want to more closely estimate expenditures on closing costs. Otherwise, for a safe ballpark estimate, assume that 10 percent of the expected sale price of your house will go toward paying closing costs.

Estimated house sale price	$ _____
– Closing costs	– $ _____
– Mortgage payoff	– $ _____
– Moving costs	– $ _____
= Estimated proceeds from house sale	= $ _____

Mortgage Payoff

For most people, the need to pay off an outstanding mortgage greatly depletes the expected proceeds from a house sale. Figuring out your mortgage payoff balance usually is a snap.

Simply review your mortgage lender's most recent monthly statement to find out the amount you still owe as of the date of the statement. You may need to make a couple of adjustments to this amount to make it more accurate.

First, on most mortgages, your outstanding balance should decline each month as you make additional payments. Because you can't sell your house immediately, your balance should decline between now and the date that you close on the sale.

Subtract from your outstanding balance the sum of the principal payments you'll be making between now and the proposed sale date. For example, if your most recent monthly mortgage statement shows that $200 of your payment went toward principal reduction, and you expect to hold onto the house for at least six more months, you can subtract $1,200 from your current outstanding balance.

_____

_____

_____

Most mortgage lenders assess a nominal fee for sending you a payoff statement detailing, to the penny, the cost of paying off your loan balance on a specific day, as well as for other paperwork fees. These fees usually don't amount to more than $100 or so, but if you want to know exactly how much to expect, simply call your lender. If the fee seems excessive or you're willing to haggle, ask the lender to reduce these fees; some will comply with your request.

Estimated house sale price	$ _____
– Closing costs	– $ _____
– Mortgage payoff	– $ _____
– Moving costs	– $ _____
= Estimated proceeds from house sale	= $ _____

Moving Expenses

Over the years, you've probably accumulated more stuff than you realize. Whether you've filled your attic with boxes of gadgets, lined your garage with old bikes, or decorated every room with the finest furnishings, you're going to have to pack up all of your belongings and have someone haul them away.

Most people don't have the equipment, experience, and muscle power to move all of their stuff themselves. If you're like most folks on the move, you call a moving service. As with any other service business, prices and quality of service vary.

The farther you move and the more weight you're moving, the more the costs escalate. Move the contents of a typical one-bedroom apartment about one-third of the way across the United States, and you can easily spend several thousands of dollars. Move the same items all the way across the country, and the cost may double. Moving the contents of a spacious four-bedroom house halfway across the country can run you $15,000 to $20,000.

Be sure to research moving costs, especially if you're selling a big house filled with furniture and other personal possessions or if you're moving a great distance. Get bids from several reputable movers and check references. Price and quality of service vary greatly.

Estimated house sale price	$ _____
– Closing costs	– $ _____
– Mortgage payoff	– $ _____
– Moving costs	– $ _____
= Estimated proceeds from house sale	= $ _____

Putting It All Together

After you understand the important elements of determining your proceeds from the expected sale of your house, you can work through the numbers to figure how much money you hope to have coming your way.

Estimated house sale price	$ _____
– Closing costs	– $ _____
– Mortgage payoff	– $ _____
– Moving costs	– $ _____
= Estimated proceeds from house sale	= $ _____

Now that you know what proceeds you can expect from your house sale, what should you do with this information? This estimate is necessary if you're at all cash constrained in buying your next home or if you're selling to finance some important financial goal, such as retirement.

11

Timing the Sale

You don't have to be a genius to get top dollar for your house when you sell it. Nor do you have to be lucky, although a little luck never hurts. If you follow the right steps *before* you put your house on the market, good fortune may come your way throughout the transaction. You can control the selling process instead of reacting to it on a crisis-by-crisis basis. You can create your own luck. This chapter shows you how to take advantage of time.

Timing the Sale of Your House

Depending on how well or how poorly you use time, it can either be an ally or a ruthless enemy during the sale.

In most communities, choosing the date that you put your house on the market is an important decision. Certain periods of each year are predictably advantageous for sellers. Others are just as predictably less than stellar.

Real estate marketing activity isn't flat throughout the year. No matter where you live in the United States, the real estate marketing calendar generally has two distinct peaks and valleys created by ebbs and flows of activity in your local real estate market (see Figure 11-1).

The sales peaks are higher and longer in good years, and the valleys are deeper and longer in bad years, but the marketing calendar's rhythm never changes. These seasonal cycles don't care about birth, death, divorce, job loss, or any other life changes that force you to sell. You can't alter the rise and fall of market cycles. You can, however, use the predictability of these cycles to your advantage. This section helps you identify when the best times are to put your house on the market and which are the worst.

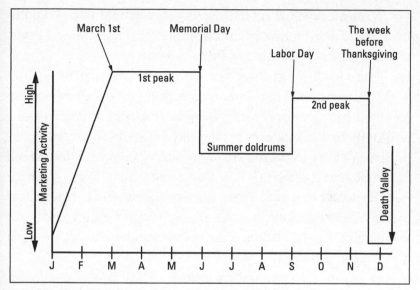

© John Wiley & Sons, Inc.

Figure 11-1: *A real estate marketing calendar usually has predictable peaks and valleys in housing sales activity.*

First peak season: Spring

Calendar years begin January 1, but real estate years don't. Depending where you live, the longer and stronger of two annual peak seasons begins somewhere between late January and early March. If you live in a temperate area, such as Florida or California, the market kicks into gear a little sooner. If you're still digging out from under ten feet of snow on March 1, your market may take a little longer to heat up.

February through May normally is the most active selling time for residential real estate. Families with children want to get their purchase or sale out of the way by late spring so moving (which typically occurs 30 to 60 days after the contract of sale is signed) won't disrupt the kids' schooling for the next academic year. Other people buy or sell early in the year for tax purposes or to avoid interference with their summer vacations. The annual outpouring of new listings pulls buyers out of the woodwork. Sellers are drawn into the market by all of the buying activity.

The first peak season is usually the best time to put your house on the market. High sale prices result from spirited buyer competition. Because more buyers are in the market now than at any other time of the year, your best chance of getting a fast, top-dollar sale is during the first season. If you intend to buy another home after yours is sold, this time period offers the best selection of homes to purchase.

_____

_____

_____

First valley: Summer

Memorial Day generally marks the beginning of the first valley. Sales activity usually slows during June, July, and August. People who bought or sold in the spring move in the summer. Buyers, sellers, and agents often take summer vacations, which reduces market activity. Many people spend their weekends having fun in the sun instead of looking at houses.

Houses ordinarily take somewhat longer to sell in the summer because of a lower level of buyer activity. Unless you have to sell now (or if property values are declining), wait until the fall to put your house on the market. You're likely to get a higher price after people return from vacation.

If you're selling your house to buy another one, keep in mind that summer is your first opportunity to go bargain shopping. Summer is a good time to find motivated sellers who bought a new home and *must* sell their old one fast before the ownership expenses of two properties put them in the poorhouse.

Second peak season: Autumn

Labor Day usually starts the second peak season. This peak normally rolls through September, October, and into November. Don't let the beautiful autumn leaves fool you, however. Just as fall brings a chill to the air, an icy edge of desperation develops in the second season for some sellers.

People who sell during late autumn tend to be *strongly* motivated. Some bought new homes in the spring before selling their old ones. Now they're slashing their asking prices after wasting months marketing overpriced property.

Others are calendar-year taxpayers who sold houses earlier in the year and want to buy their new home on or before December 31. Why? So they can pay tax-deductible expenses (such as the loan origination fee, mortgage interest, and property taxes) before the end of the year to reduce the impact of federal and state income tax. Either way, these folks are under pressure to sell.

If you're a bit of a gambler, the second peak season may be the most rewarding time to sell. Given that you correctly apply the pricing techniques we describe in Chapter 12, your house should sell quickly and profitably. Unless prices are rapidly increasing in your

area, wait until activity slows in mid-November and
then buy your next home at a discount price. You get
the best of both worlds — "sell high and buy low."

Deciding to sell during the second peak season can be a
risky gambit. If you inadvertently overprice your house, it
won't sell. If you need to sell, carefully monitor buyer response
to your property. Be prepared to drop your asking price. Don't
wait until Thanksgiving to reduce your price. You may end up
attempting to sell your house during the dreaded dead season
(see the following section).

Second Valley: Winter

The second peak season usually comes to a screeching halt a
week or two before Thanksgiving. With the exception of a few,
mostly desperate, sellers and bargain-hunting or relocating
buyers who stay in the market until the end of December, residential real estate sales activity ordinarily slows significantly
by mid-November. People stop buying property and start buying gifts. Would-be sellers take their houses off the market.

The end of the year is generally the worst time of year to
sell a house. The weather may be miserable, and very few

buyers are in the market. Time will show you no mercy if you wait until this point to get realistic about pricing your house to sell. Don't put your house on the market during November and December unless you have absolutely no other alternative.

Timing the Purchase of Your Home

So which comes first, selling your house before buying a new one, or buying first and then selling? Neither course of action is risk free. The adverse consequences of buying a new home before selling your present house, however, can be far more dire. At worst, buying your dream house before selling your present house may put you in the poorhouse. However, you can make a compelling case for either course of action:

- **Selling before you buy eliminates financial risk.** When you sell first, you know precisely how much money you have from your sale to put toward your next home. No sleepless nights worrying about how you'll come up with the cash you need for a down payment on your new home or how much longer you'll have to make mortgage, property tax, and insurance payments on two houses. Your fiscal future is clear.

- **Selling first, however, introduces uncertainties and problems.** If you sell first, you may be forced out of your old house before you have somewhere else to go. Where will you live? Where will your kids go to school? Do you really want to move twice? What if you can't find a home you like as much as the one you just sold? Putting your life on hold while searching for a new home is emotionally draining and insomnia producing.

Given a choice between either selling your present house first *or* buying your next home first, we strongly recommend that you sell your present house before purchasing a new home. Even in good real estate markets, sales frequently drag on much longer than you expect. Selling in a weak market usually compounds the problem. Homeowners tend to overestimate their house's resale value and underestimate the length of the selling process — a fiscally deadly one-two punch.

12

Pricing to Sell

If you *really* want to be a successful seller, think like a buyer. You probably didn't buy the first house you looked at. Few folks do. On the contrary, most people spend months industriously inspecting many houses on the market. To avoid overpaying for the home they ultimately purchase, buyers are forced to become experts on property values.

You can ask any price you want for your house, but your house won't sell until you find a buyer who agrees that it's worth the price you're willing to accept. Smart sellers know that although only *one* person sets a price, *two* people — a seller and a buyer — make a sale.

Adverse factors outside of your control (such as a flood of houses on the market, high mortgage interest rates, or dismal consumer confidence) may negatively affect your sale price.

However, you can create demand for your house, no matter how poor prevailing market conditions are. This chapter shows you how.

Cost, Price, and Value

Many people use *cost, price,* and *value* interchangeably; however, the three terms mean very different things. This linguistic imprecision creates big problems during negotiations between buyers and sellers.

The fact is, neither *cost* nor *price* is the same as *value.* After you understand the meanings of these words and how they differ, you can say exactly what you mean and replace emotion with objectivity during price negotiations.

Value is elusive

Value is your opinion of your house's worth to you based on the way you use it now and plan to use it in the future. Note that, in the preceding sentence, the words "your" and "you" each appear twice. Because *your* opinion is subjective, the features *you* value may not be the features that someone else values.

You may, for example, believe that the only acceptable house color is beet red. Someone else may feel just as strongly that only sky blue houses are gorgeous. No harm done, as long as everyone realizes that a big difference exists between opinions and facts.

Two factors greatly affect value:

- **Internal factors:** Your personal (internal) situation changes over time. Suppose that 30 years ago, when you bought your present house, you put great value on a four-bedroom home with a fenced-in backyard. The house had to be located in a terrific school system. Why? Because 30 years ago, you were the proud parent of two adorable children.

  Now your children are grown and have their own homes. Without kids, you don't need the big house, huge yard, or terrific school system. The house didn't change — what changed were the internal factors regarding your use for the house and, thus, its value to you. Divorce and retirement are other examples of internal factors that compel folks to buy or sell houses.

- **External factors:** Circumstances outside of your control that affect property values also change for better or worse. If, for example, commute time to the city where you work is cut from 1 hour to 30 minutes when mass transit rail service is extended into your area, your house's value increases. If, on the other hand, a toxic waste dump is discovered next to your house, the house's value takes a hit.

The law of supply and demand is another external factor that affects value. If more people want to buy houses than sell them, buyer competition drives up house prices. If, on the other hand, more people want to sell than buy, reduced demand results in lower property prices.

Cost is history

Cost measures past expenditures — for example, the amount you originally paid for your house. The amount you paid long ago, or the amount you spent fixing up the house after you bought it, doesn't mean a thing as far as your house's present or future value is concerned.

For example, when home prices began skyrocketing in many areas of the country during the early 2000s, some buyers accused sellers of being greedy. "You paid $75,000 fifteen years ago. Now you're asking $250,000," they said. "That's a huge profit."

"So what?" sellers replied. "If you don't want to pay our modest asking price, move out of the way so the nice buyers standing behind you can present their offers." In a hot sellers' market, people who base their offering prices on the original price paid for a property waste everyone's time.

The market can change radically in a few short years. By 2008–09 in the midst of the Great Recession, prices had declined dramatically in many areas. Sellers would have been ecstatic to find buyers willing to pay them the amount they'd paid less than five years earlier when home prices peaked. In those areas, sellers who priced their houses based on the inflated purchase prices they'd paid years earlier learned a painful lesson: Your potential profit *or loss* as a seller doesn't enter into the equation when determining your house's present value.

Price is the here and now

You put an *asking* price on your house. Buyers put an *offering* price in their contract. You and the buyers negotiate back and forth to establish your house's *purchase* price. Today's purchase price becomes tomorrow's cost.

_____

_____

_____

Cost is the past, price is the present, and value is in the eye of the beholder. Neither the price you paid for your house years ago when you bought it nor the amount you want to get for it today matters to buyers. Don't waste valuable time on fantasy pricing.

Fair Market Value (FMV)

Every house sells at the right price. That price is defined as its *fair market value* (FMV) — the price a buyer will pay and a seller will accept for the house — given that neither buyer nor seller is under duress. Duress comes from life changes, such as divorce or sudden job transfer, that put either the buyer or seller under pressure to perform quickly. If appraisers know that a sale was made under duress, they raise or lower the sale price accordingly to more accurately reflect the house's true FMV.

FMV is much more powerful than plain old *value*. Sellers have an opinion about the amount their house is worth. Buyers have a separate, not necessarily equal, and probably lower, opinion of the same house's value. Values are opinions, not facts.

FMV, conversely, is fact. It becomes fact the moment the seller and the buyer agree on a mutually acceptable price. Just as it takes two to tango, it takes a seller and a buyer to make FMV. Facts are bankable.

Need-based pricing isn't FMV

Whenever the residential real estate market gets soft, many would-be sellers feel that FMV isn't fair at all. "Why doesn't our house sell?" they ask. "Why can't we get our asking price? It's not fair."

Don't confuse "fair" with equitable or favorable. Despite its amiable name, FMV is brutally impartial and sometimes even cruel. Need is not an integral component of FMV. FMV doesn't give a hoot about any of the following:

- How much money you *need* because you overpaid for your house when you bought it
- How much money you *need* to replace the money you spent fixing up your house after you bought it
- How much money you *need* to pay off your mortgage or home-equity loan
- How much money you *need* from the sale to buy your next home

Here's why *need* doesn't determine FMV. Suppose two identical houses located next door to one another are listed for sale at the same time. One house was purchased by Maria for $30,000 in 1990. You made a $60,000 cash down payment when you bought the other house for $300,000 two years ago. As luck would have it, property values declined a year after you bought your house.

You clearly *need* more money from the sale than Maria. After all, you paid ten times as much for your house. What's more, Maria paid off her loan five years ago. You, on the other hand, owe the bank big bucks on your mortgage.

Because the houses are identical in size, age, condition, and location, they have the same FMV. Under the circumstances, the fact that they both sold for $285,000 isn't surprising. Maria got a nice nest egg for her retirement. You barely cleared enough from the deal to pay off your mortgage and other expenses of sale. Fair? Maria thinks so. You don't.

FMV is utterly unbiased. It's the amount your house is worth in the market today — not the amount you or the buyers would like it to be.

Median prices aren't FMV

Organizations such as the National Association of Realtors, the Chamber of Commerce, and private research firms gather data on house sales activity in a specific geographic region, such as a city, county, or state. They use this information to prepare reports on housing topics, such as the average cost of houses in an area and the increase or decline in regional house sales on a yearly or monthly basis.

One of the most widely quoted housing statistics is the *median sale price,* which is simply the midpoint in a range of all house sales in an area during a specified reporting period, such as a month or a year. Half the sales during the reporting period are above the median, and half fall below it.

The median-priced house, in other words, is the one exactly in the middle of the prices of all the houses that sold during the specified reporting period.

For example, the median sale price of an existing single-family house in the United States was about $265,000 in 2017 — meaning that half the houses in the United States sold for more than $265,000 and the other half sold for less than $265,000. Unfortunately, all you know about this hypothetical median-priced American house is its price.

You don't know how many bedrooms or baths the mythical median-priced house contains. Nor do you know how many square feet of interior living space the house offers, how old it is, whether it has a garage or a yard, or how well maintained it is. You don't even know where in the United States this elusive median-priced house is located.

As a homeowner, you can use median sale price statistics to measure *general* property value trends. For example, suppose your local Chamber of Commerce says the median sale price of a house in your area was $200,000 five years ago when you bought your house, and it's $240,000 today. Based on that information, you can safely say that median sale prices have increased 20 percent over the past five years.

Just because the median sale price of a house in your area went up 20 percent doesn't mean the house you paid $250,000 for five years ago is worth $300,000 today. Median sale price statistics aren't any more accurate for determining your house's value than median income statistics are for calculating your paycheck. You need much more precise information to establish the FMV of the house you're about to sell.

Comparable Market Analysis

The best way to accurately determine your house's FMV is by using a written *comparable market analysis* (CMA) to see how your house compares to other houses like yours that have either sold recently or currently are on the market. If you hire a real estate agent to sell your house and use the techniques we cover in Chapter 3 to select your agent, you get several CMAs during the selection process. You can use these CMAs to fine-tune your asking price.

Every residential real estate office develops its own CMA format. Regardless of the way your agent's office presents its CMA information, all good CMAs contain two sections, and those sections contain additional details:

- Recent Sales
  - Address
  - Date sold
  - Sale price
  - Bedrooms/bathrooms
  - Parking
  - Condition
  - Remarks

- Currently For Sale
  - Address
  - Date on market
  - Asking price
  - Bedrooms/bathrooms
  - Parking
  - Condition
  - Remarks

The "Recent Sales" section of the CMA helps establish the FMV of *your house* by comparing it to all other houses that

- Are located in the same neighborhood as your house
- Are of approximately the same age, size, and condition as your house
- Have sold in the past six months

Houses meeting these criteria are called *comps*, which is short for *comparables*. Depending on the date you started looking at houses for sale in your neighborhood, you may not have visited all the sold comps. No problem. A good real estate agent can show you listing statements for the houses you haven't seen, take you on a verbal tour of every house, and explain how each one compares with your house.

The "Currently For Sale" section of the CMA compares your house to neighborhood comps that are *currently on the market*. These comps are included in the analysis to check price trends. If prices are falling, asking prices of houses on the market today will be lower than sale prices of comparable houses. If prices are rising, you'll see higher asking prices today than sale prices for comps that sold three to six months ago.

When you analyze the data in a comp, you may see a note about the price per square foot for each house listed. Putting the sale prices into a *price-per-square-foot format* makes property comparisons much easier. Any price that's way above or below the norm leaps out at you.

Pricing Methods

You can pick a price for your house in a hundred different ways — pay for a professional appraisal, grab a number out of your hat, interview dozens of real estate agents until you find one with a suitably elevated opinion of your house's value, and so on. In the final analysis, however, they're all variations of the two pricing methods we discuss in the following sections.

Four-phase pricing: Ineffective

The consequences of pulling an unsubstantiated asking price out of the air are unacceptable for a smart seller. You may undervalue your house and risk leaving money on the table when you sell. Or, more likely, you may overprice your house, which results in an exhaustingly slow marketing process that ultimately lowers your sale price. Houses marketed by unrealistic sellers usually go through the following four distinct pricing phases prior to sale:

- **Phase one:** Sellers start by blithely disregarding any factual pricing method, such as checking comparable property sales, aka comps. Why? Some sellers don't know any better or get lousy advice from their real estate agents. Other sellers think their house is superior to those ticky-tacky comps. Either way, this misguided method generally results in grotesque overpricing.

- **Phase two:** After several months of market rejection, the sellers grudgingly make a tiny price reduction, which brings their asking price down from the grotesque level to merely overpriced.

- **Phase three:** More lonely months pass, and then two things happen. First, the sellers typically get a new agent. Second, the sellers reduce their asking price to one that "leaves room to negotiate." Even though the revised price still is moderately higher than the house's probable sale price based on sales of comparable property, at least the new asking price has some basis in market reality.

- **Phase four:** The sellers ultimately accept the validity of comps and reduce their asking price accordingly to a "let's sell it" level. After the sellers establish a good correlation between asking price and fair market value (FMV), their house *finally* sells.

Ironically, instead of getting more money with this method, four-phase pricing usually stigmatizes a property and reduces the eventual sale price to *less* than it would've been with more realistic pricing. Here's why:

- **The listing agent can't justify an indefensible asking price.** If the asking price has no factual basis, the agent can't provide a good answer to buyers who ask, "Why hasn't the house sold after all this time on the market? What's *wrong* with it?"

_____

_____

_____

- **The property is slowly but surely buried by new listings that come on the market.** After several months, most buyers and agents either forget that your house still is on the market or belittle the house by saying, "That old thing. It'll never sell." In desperation, sellers are forced to slash their asking price to the bone to attract buyers.

Four-phase pricing creates a self-fulfilling prophecy. Folks who use this pricing method expect it will take a long time to sell their house. In a strong market, they're correct because the market will ultimately rise to their price level. In a weak market, they're disastrously correct as they chase the market ever lower.

Pleasure-pleasure-panic pricing: Top-dollar sales

The smart way to sell your property is the pleasure-pleasure-panic pricing method. You can sell your house quickly *and* get the highest possible price by using this method. The secret of success is establishing a realistic asking price for your house when you first place it on the market.

_____

_____

_____

The correct way to establish an asking price is to analyze houses comparable to yours in size, age, condition, and location — houses that currently are on the market and those that have sold within the past six months. Don't be misled by asking prices; many sellers use four-phase pricing. *Sale prices*, not asking prices, determine fair market value.

Here's how the pleasure-pleasure-panic pricing method works — Milt and Judy have spent the last three months looking at houses on the market in their price range. They're educated buyers; they know how to distinguish between a well-priced house and an overpriced property.

Judy and Milt nearly bought a great house a couple of months ago. It had all the features they wanted and was fairly priced. However, Milt didn't realize how well priced it was because he'd just started the education process. While Milt was haggling over the price and terms of sale, the seller accepted a better offer.

They're spending today the same way they've spent the previous 11 Sundays, touring what seems like an endless series of newly listed overpriced properties with their agent. Then Judy and Milt trudge into your *first* open house and pleasure-pleasure-panic kicks into gear.

- **Pleasure Number 1:** Judy and Milt love your property. It's the best place they've seen in the past three months. They could live in your house happily ever after. Their eyes start to sparkle.

- **Pleasure Number 2:** Milt and Judy can't believe their eyes when they look at the asking price on your listing statement. By now, they know property values every bit as well as their agent. Your house is definitely priced to sell. Their hands start to tremble.

- **Panic:** Judy and Milt see another couple entering your house. They've seen these folks at many other open houses during the past couple of months. That familiarity isn't a coincidence. The other couple obviously wants to buy a house in the same neighborhood and price range.

Judy and Milt stare at each other in horror. If they love your house and know that it's well priced, so will the other couple. They realize that if they don't act quickly, the other couple will snap up the house. Milt tells their agent to write up a full-asking-price offer. Judy instructs the agent to go $10,000 above your asking price just to be safe. Milt agrees. He doesn't want to be a two-time loser.

That scenario explains how pleasure-pleasure-panic pricing creates a seller's market even in the midst of a buyer's market. This approach puts intense pressure on buyers to perform quickly.

Don't be surprised if you get several purchase offers, including some that are equal to or more than full asking price, as soon as your house hits the market — if your house is priced right. After your property has been given broad, immediate market exposure, spirited competition forces buyers to pay top dollar for your house. This method works almost every time.

Quantum pricing: An effective technique

Put yourself in the buyer's shoes for a moment and imagine that you're buying, not selling, your house. If you're like most people, one of the first things you do is decide how much you want to spend. For example, you set your upper limit of affordability at $250,000. If you're working with a real estate agent, you probably tell the agent, "I don't want to spend more than $250,000," or "Don't show me anything that costs more than $250,000." Why waste time looking at property you can't afford to buy?

Buyers use price limits, called *quantums*, to simplify house hunting. Pricing quantums are initially expressed in nice, round, easy-to-work-with numbers, such as $100,000 and $50,000, and then fine-tuned to $25,000 and $10,000 quantums.

Think of buyers as fish swimming in an ocean of houses for sale. At any given time, huge schools of buyer-fish usually are swimming in this sea. However, the buyer-fish swim at many different levels; one school swims at the $150,000-to-$200,000 price quantum level, another swims at the $200,000-to-$250,000 price quantum level, and so on.

Buyer-fish from higher-price quantums occasionally swim down to a lower quantum in their searches for a house. However, buyer-fish rarely swim up to a higher quantum (if they establish realistic affordability limits). When a buyer-fish can't afford to swim *up,* the price must drop *down* to the buyer-fish's price quantum for the house to sell.

Establishing price quantums

Follow these steps to use price quantums to hone your initial asking price to pleasure-pleasure-panic perfection:

1. **Determine your house's market value within the appropriate $100,000 quantum, unless you happen to live in an area where no house ever has sold for more than $99,999.99.**

   Use the comparable market analysis (CMA) method to define a general price range for your property. For example, if a CMA shows that five houses similar to yours in size, age, condition, and location sold within the past six months for $310,000 to $335,000, your house belongs in the $300,000 to $400,000 quantum.

2. **Adjust the price within the correct $50,000 quantum.**

   Continuing with the same example, decide whether your asking price should be over or under $350,000. Because not one of the comps sold for more than $335,000, your price belongs in the $300,000 to $350,000 quantum.

3. **Fine-tune your price to the closest $25,000 quantum.**

   The more accurate your pricing, the more exacting your scrutiny. Deciding whether the price should be in the $300,000 to $325,000 quantum or the $325,000 to $350,000 quantum requires careful analysis. If, for example, four of the five comps sold between $310,000 and $325,000 and the fifth went for $335,000, you'd be wise to keep the asking price under $325,000.

4. **Ultrafine-tune your price to the nearest $10,000 quantum.**

This is the moment of truth. Now you must decide on the *precise* point between $310,000 and $325,000 to put your price. If the actual prices of comparable houses that sold under $325,000 were $310,000, $317,500, $319,500, and $322,000, three out of four sales point toward an asking price under $320,000.

Recognizing quantum-pricing finesse points

If you seriously want to sell quickly for top dollar, don't put your asking price in the next higher quantum to give yourself "room to negotiate." Here's why:

- **Excitement:** It takes courage to price your house a hair *below* the nearest price quantum (rather than above

the quantum, so you have room to negotiate down-
ward). For example, suppose that the comps indicate
a probable sale near $250,000. A $249,500 asking price
may create enough buyer excitement to generate multiple purchase offers that push your sale price higher
than the asking price. Price your property at $269,500 to
give yourself a $20,000 negotiating cushion, and your
house is just another yawner.

- **Computers:** All agents use computers tied to their
multiple listing service's (MLS) database to perform
property searches. For example, a buyer decides on a
neighborhood and asks the agent for a list of homes
with the following features: three bedrooms, two-and-
a-half baths, a two-car garage, and an asking price of
$250,000 or less. Per the agent's request, the MLS com-
puter spews out listings that meet these conditions.
The computer isn't smart enough to make allowances
for properties with negotiating room in their prices.
If your house is listed at $269,500 or even $251,500, it
won't be on the printout, and buyers won't know it
exists.

Some agents show buyers higher-priced houses they think will sell in the buyers' price range because the asking prices are "soft." Smart agents, however, know that buyers are deeply concerned about being manipulated into purchasing a more costly house. These agents won't show buyers property over the stated price limit until the buyers have seen every house on the market in their specified price range and requested to see more expensive homes.

Less buyer exposure to your house means less buyer competition for it. Less competition translates into a longer time on the market — and usually a lower sale price. High sale prices come from spirited buyer competition.

- **Conditioning:** Whether people are buying houses or blouses, everyone loves a bargain. Believe it or not, *$9.95 advertising* is mighty effective. A nickel isn't much, but most people are conditioned to think that $9.95 is much cheaper than $10. Subconsciously, $249,500 is more exciting than $250,000, and $299,950 sounds like a much better deal than $300,000. Don't try to buck a lifetime of Pavlovian conditioning; smart pricing makes buyers drool.

Don't price your property to dazzle your pals. You may impress people by telling them that you're asking $300,000 for your house, but that's a foolish price compared to $299,950. Price your house to sell, not to feed your ego.

About the Authors

Eric Tyson is a syndicated personal financial writer, lecturer, and counselor. He is dedicated to teaching people to manage their personal finances better. Eric is a former management consultant to Fortune 500 financial service firms. Over the past two decades, he has successfully invested in securities as well as in real estate, and started and managed several growing businesses. He earned a bachelor's degree in economics at Yale and an MBA at the Stanford Graduate School of Business.

Ray Brown is a veteran of the real estate profession with more than four decades of hands-on experience. He is a former manager for Coldwell Banker Residential Brokerage Company, McGuire Real Estate, and Pacific Union GMAC Real Estate, and he founded his own real estate firm, the Raymond Brown Company. Ray is also a writer, consultant, and public speaker on residential real estate topics.